Believe me. they won't mind if you drag the ham off the table... would I lie to you?
Psych
tties

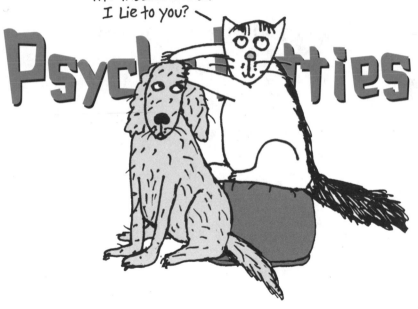

OTHER BOOKS
BY NICOLE HOLLANDER

My Cat's Not Fat, He's Just Big-Boned

Everything Here Is Mine

Psycho Kitties

by Nicole Hollander

SOURCEBOOKS HYSTERIA™
AN IMPRINT OF SOURCEBOOKS, INC.®
NAPERVILLE, ILLINOIS

Published by Sourcebooks, Inc.
P.O. Box 4410
Naperville, Illinois 60567-4410
(630) 961-3900
FAX: (630) 961-2168
www.sourcebooks.com

ISBN-13: 978-1-4022-0729-7
ISBN-10: 1-4022-0729-8

Printed and bound in the United States of America
CG 10 9 8 7 6 5 4 3 2 1

This book is Dedicated to
my own beloved psycho kitties:
Buddy and Sally Cookie

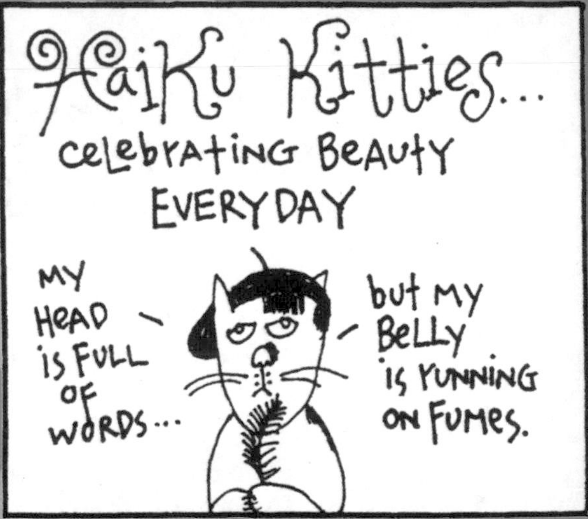
Haiku Kitties...
celebrating Beauty
EVERYDAY
MY HEAD is FULL OF WORDS...
but MY BeLLY is running ON FUMes.

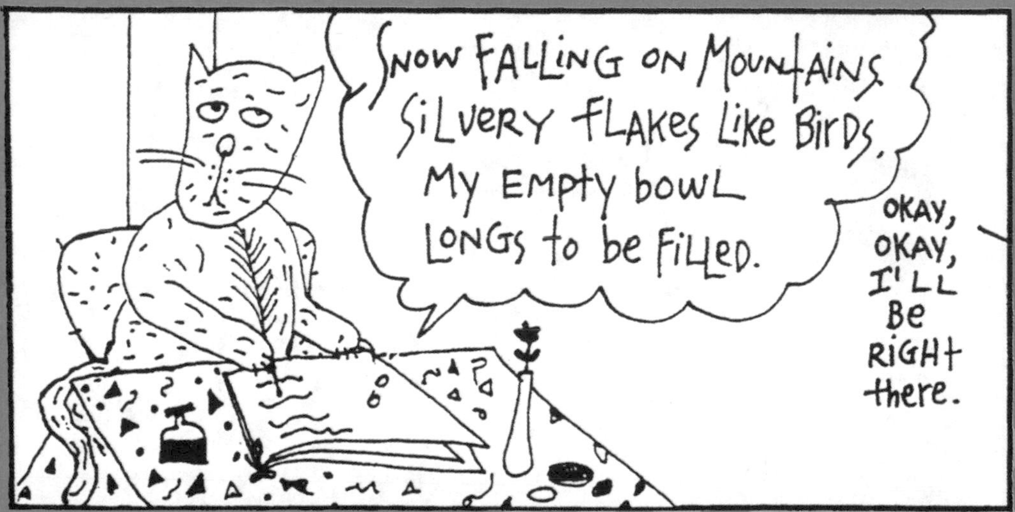
SNOW FALLING ON MOUNTAINS.
SILVERY FLAKES LIKE BIRDS.
MY EMPTY BOWL
LONGS TO BE FILLED.
OKAY, OKAY, I'LL BE RIGHT THERE.

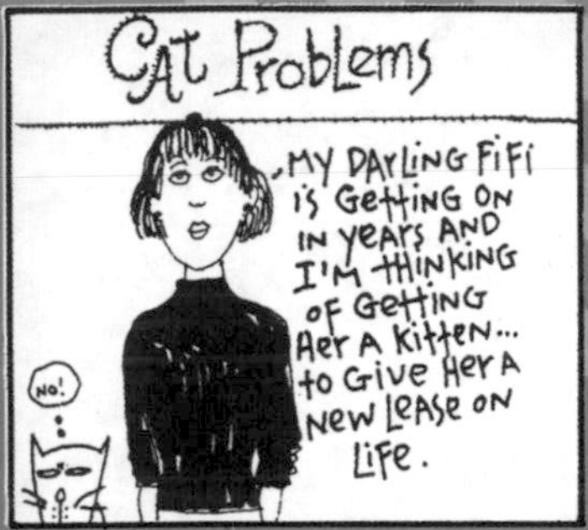
Cat Problems
My darling Fifi is getting on in years and I'm thinking of getting her a kitten... to give her a new lease on life.
No!

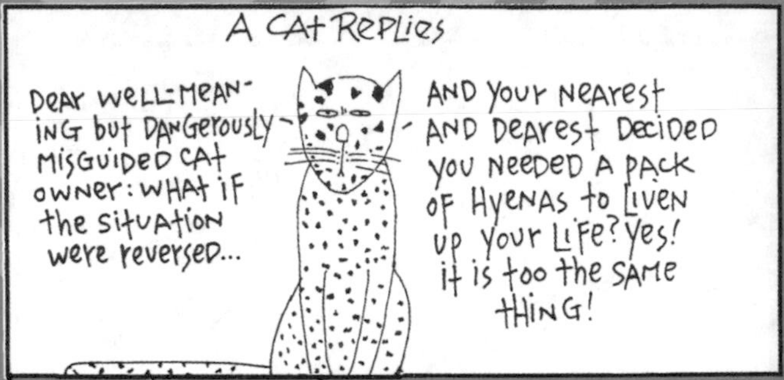
A Cat Replies
Dear well-meaning but dangerously misguided cat owner: what if the situation were reversed...
And your nearest and dearest decided you needed a pack of hyenas to liven up your life? Yes! It is too the same thing!

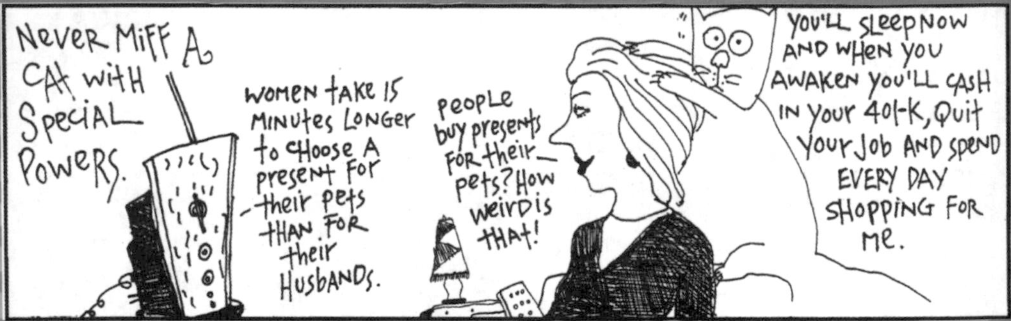
Never Miff a Cat with Special Powers.
Women take 15 minutes longer to choose a present for their pets than for their husbands.
People buy presents for their pets? How weird is that!
You'll sleep now and when you awaken you'll cash in your 401-K, quit your job and spend every day shopping for me.

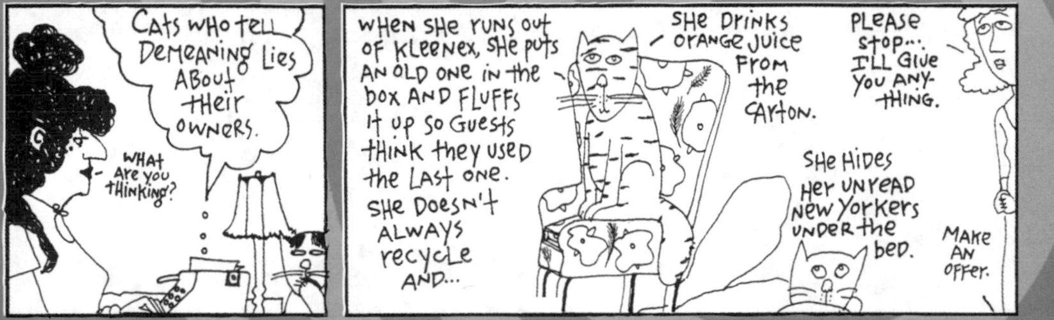
CATS WHO TELL DEMEANING LIES ABOUT THEIR OWNERS.
WHAT ARE YOU THINKING?
WHEN SHE RUNS OUT OF KLEENEX, SHE PUTS AN OLD ONE IN THE BOX AND FLUFFS IT UP SO GUESTS THINK THEY USED THE LAST ONE. SHE DOESN'T ALWAYS RECYCLE AND...
SHE DRINKS ORANGE JUICE FROM THE CARTON.
PLEASE STOP... I'LL GIVE YOU ANYTHING.
SHE HIDES HER UNREAD NEW YORKERS UNDER THE BED.
MAKE AN OFFER.

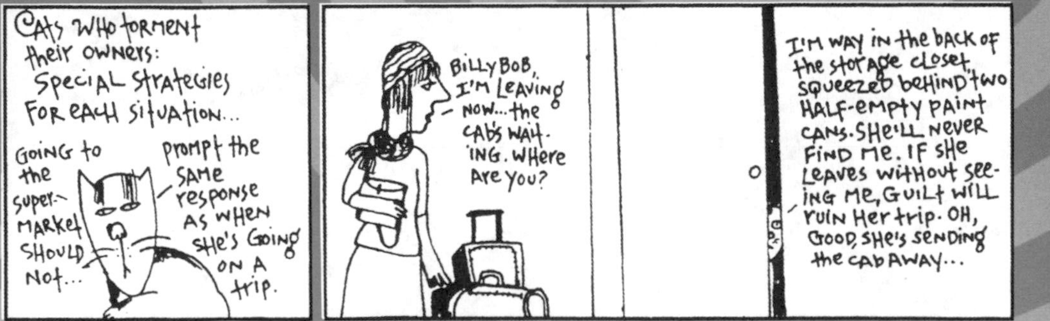
CATS WHO TORMENT THEIR OWNERS: SPECIAL STRATEGIES FOR EACH SITUATION...
GOING TO THE SUPERMARKET SHOULD NOT...
PROMPT THE SAME RESPONSE AS WHEN SHE'S GOING ON A TRIP.
BILLY BOB, I'M LEAVING NOW... THE CAB'S WAITING. WHERE ARE YOU?
I'M WAY IN THE BACK OF THE STORAGE CLOSET, SQUEEZED BEHIND TWO HALF-EMPTY PAINT CANS. SHE'LL NEVER FIND ME. IF SHE LEAVES WITHOUT SEEING ME, GUILT WILL RUIN HER TRIP. OH, GOOD, SHE'S SENDING THE CAB AWAY...

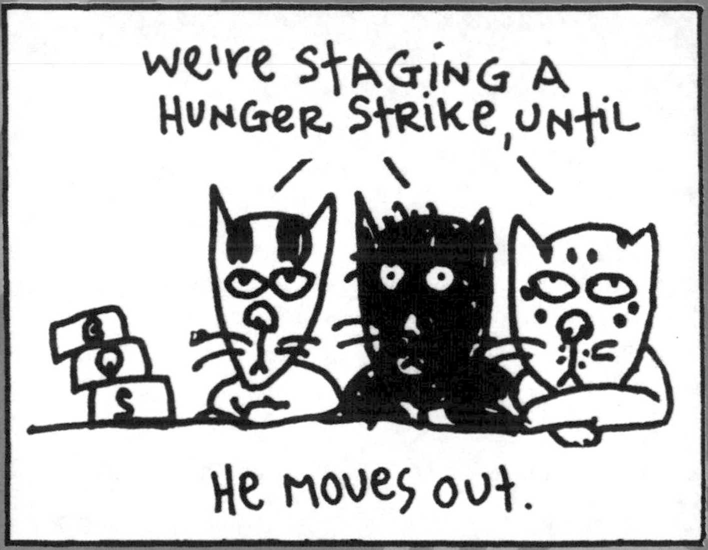
WE'RE STAGING A HUNGER STRIKE, UNTIL
HE MOVES OUT.

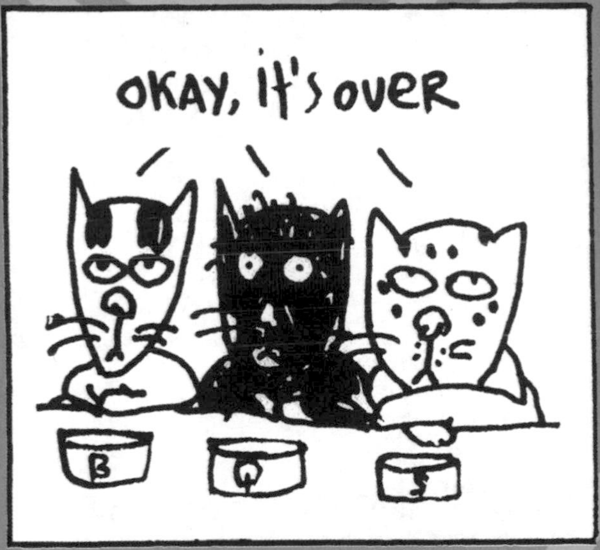
OKAY, it's OVER

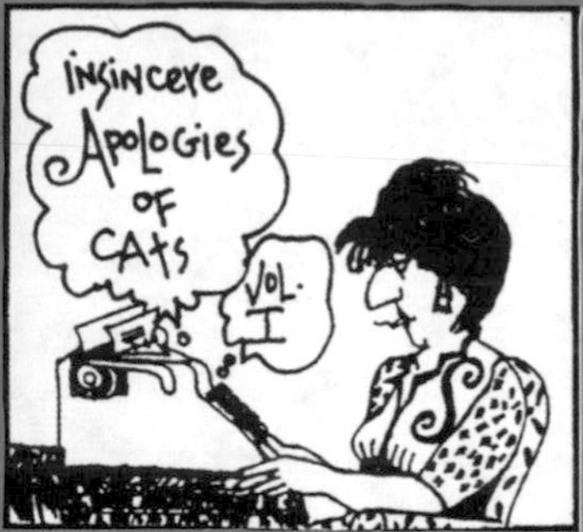
Insincere Apologies of Cats
Vol. I

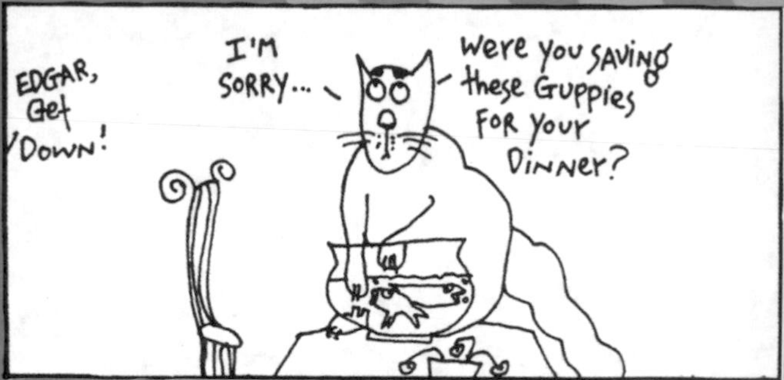
EDGAR, Get Down!
I'M SORRY...
Were you saving these Guppies for your Dinner?

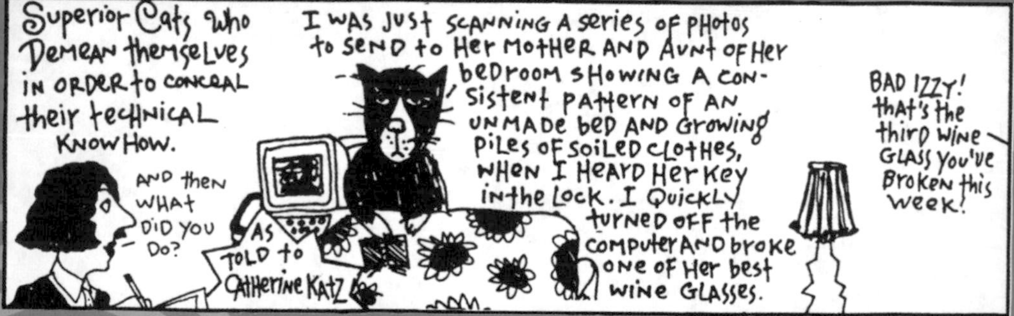
Superior Cats who Demean themselves in order to conceal their technical know how.
And then what did you do?
I was just scanning a series of photos to send to her mother and aunt of her bedroom showing a consistent pattern of an unmade bed and growing piles of soiled clothes, when I heard her key in the lock. I quickly turned off the computer and broke one of her best wine glasses.
As told to Catherine Katz
Bad Izzy! that's the third wine glass you've broken this week!

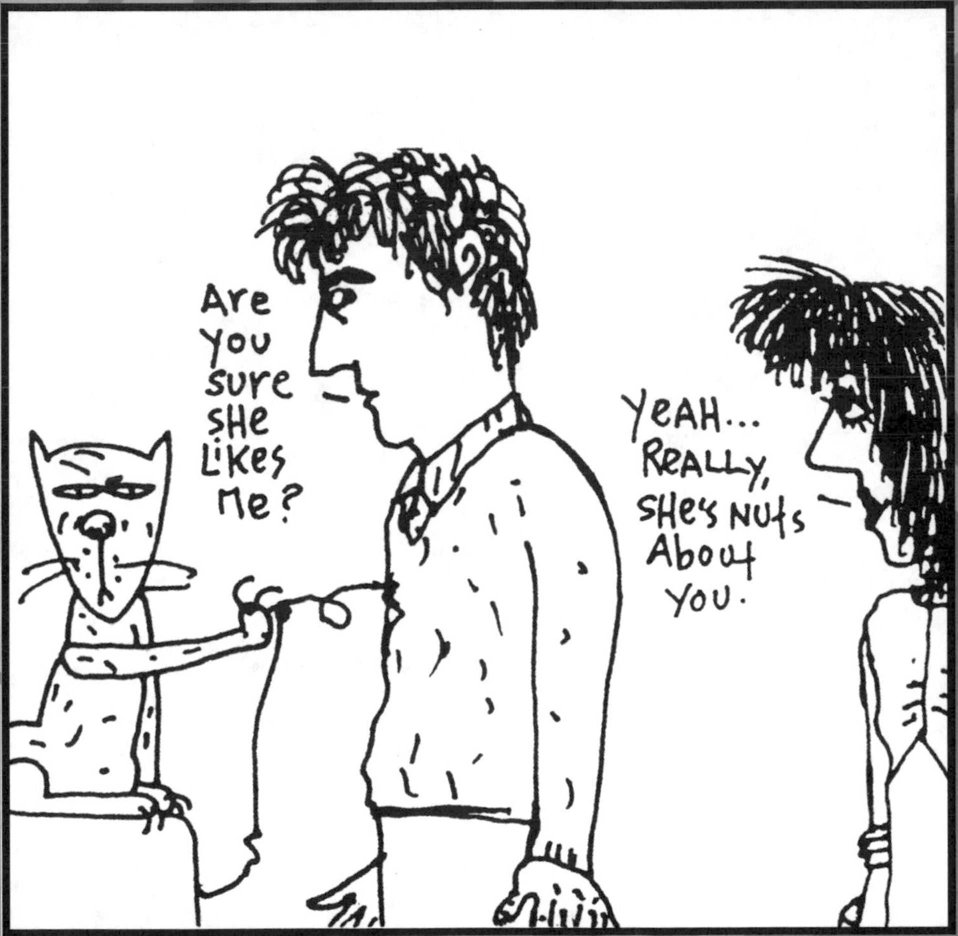
Are you sure she likes me?
Yeah... Really, she's nuts about you.

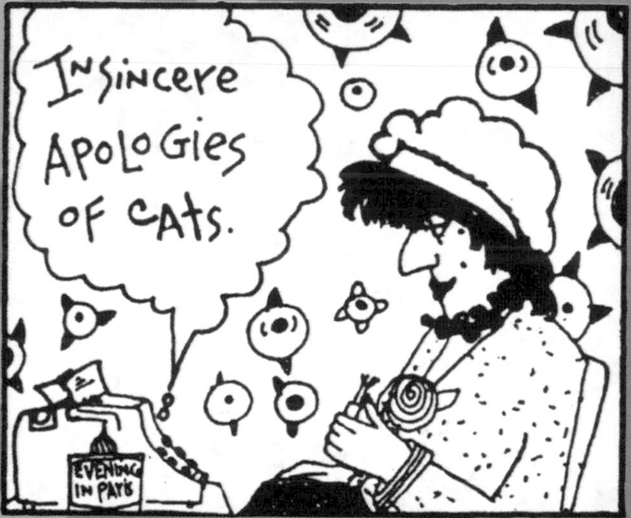
INSINCERE APOLOGIES OF CATS.
EVENING IN PARIS

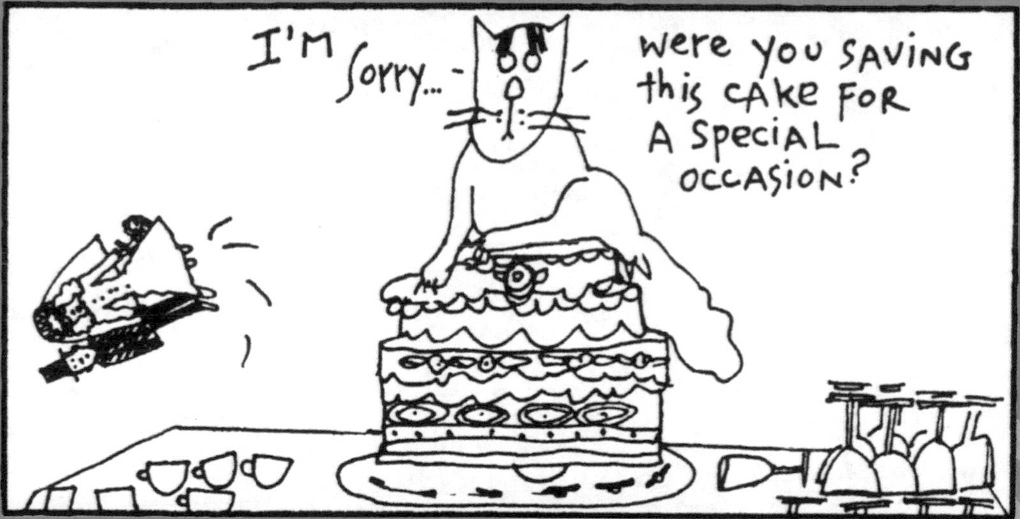
I'M sorry...
were you SAVING this CAKE FOR A Special OCCASION?

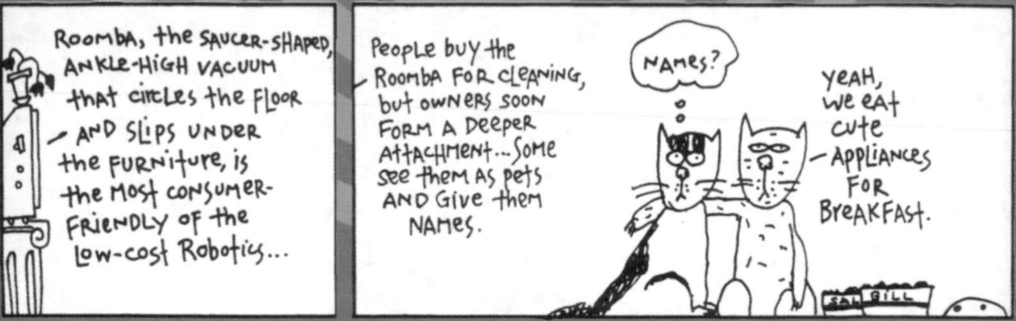
Roomba, the saucer-shaped, ankle-high vacuum that circles the floor and slips under the furniture, is the most consumer-friendly of the low-cost robotics...
People buy the Roomba for cleaning, but owners soon form a deeper attachment... Some see them as pets and give them names.
Names?
Yeah, we eat cute appliances for breakfast.
SAL
BILL

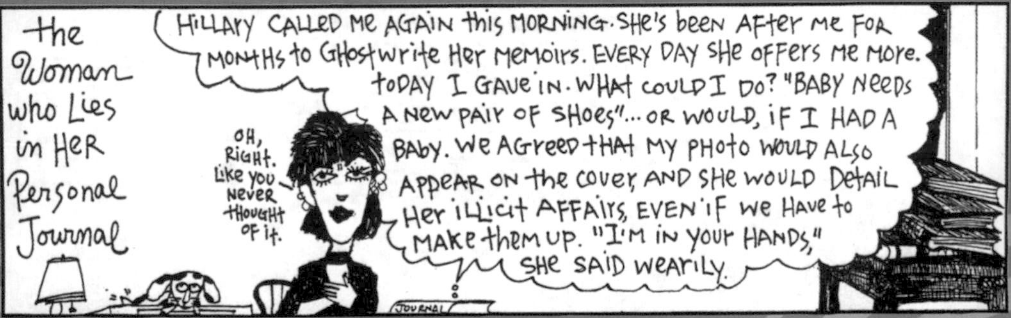
the Woman who Lies in Her Personal Journal
Hillary called me again this morning. She's been after me for months to ghostwrite her memoirs. Every day she offers me more. Today I gave in. What could I do? "Baby needs a new pair of shoes"... or would, if I had a baby. We agreed that my photo would also appear on the cover, and she would detail her illicit affairs, even if we have to make them up. "I'm in your hands," she said wearily.
Oh, right. Like you never thought of it.
JOURNAL

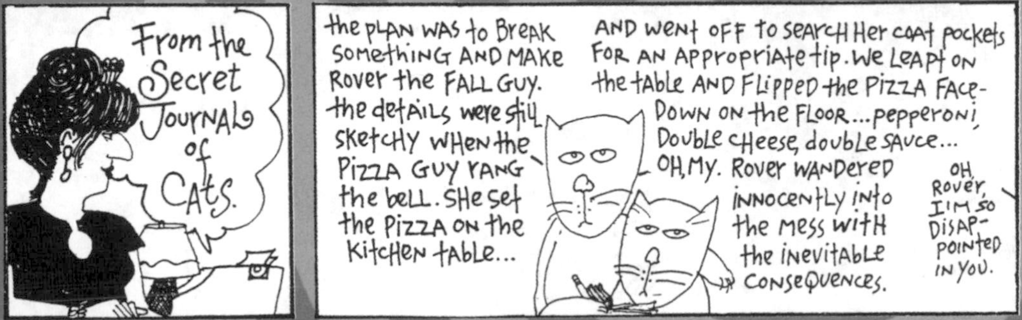
From the Secret Journal of Cats.
the plan was to break something and make Rover the fall guy. the details were still sketchy when the pizza guy rang the bell. She set the pizza on the kitchen table...
and went off to search her coat pockets for an appropriate tip. We leapt on the table and flipped the pizza face-down on the floor...pepperoni, double cheese, double sauce... Oh, my. Rover wandered innocently into the mess with the inevitable consequences.
Oh, Rover, I'm so disappointed in you.

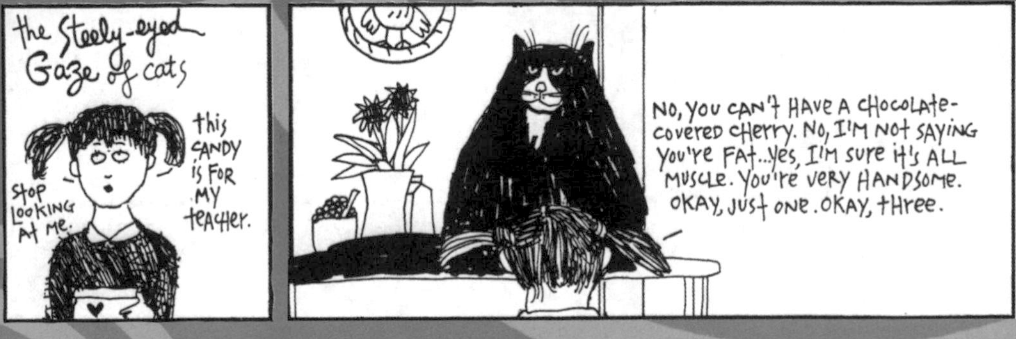
the Steely-eyed Gaze of cats
this candy is for my teacher.
Stop looking at me.
No, you can't have a chocolate-covered cherry. No, I'm not saying you're fat...yes, I'm sure it's all muscle. You're very handsome. Okay, just one. Okay, three.

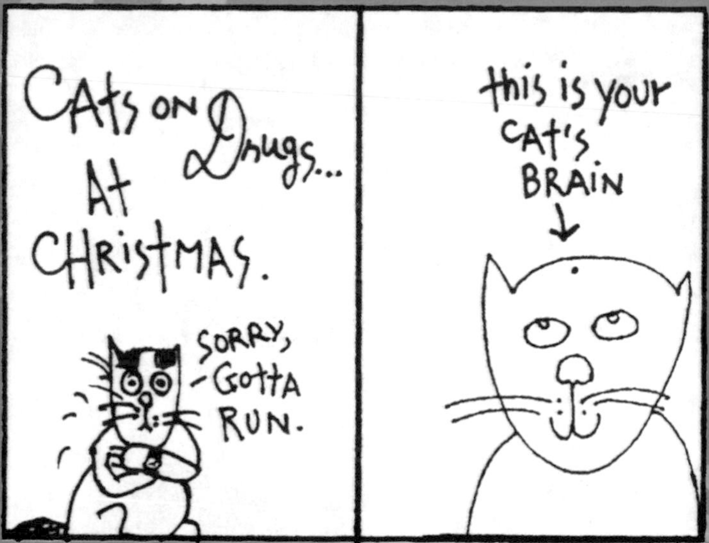

Cats on Drugs...
At
Christmas.
Sorry,
-Gotta
Run.
this is your
cat's
brain

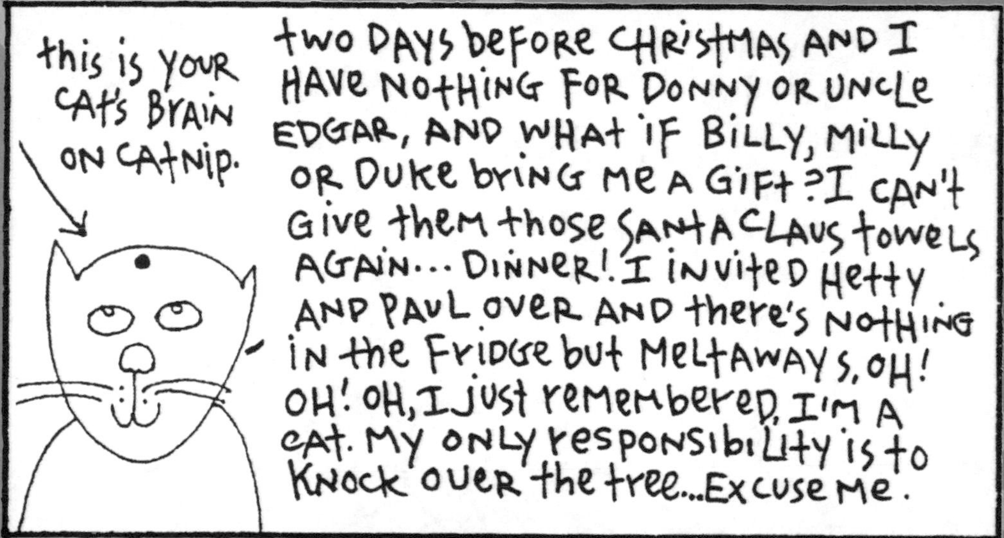
this is your cat's brain on catnip.
two days before Christmas and I have nothing for Donny or Uncle Edgar, and what if Billy, Milly or Duke bring me a gift? I can't give them those Santa Claus towels again... Dinner! I invited Hetty and Paul over and there's nothing in the fridge but Meltaways. Oh! Oh! Oh, I just remembered, I'm a cat. My only responsibility is to knock over the tree...Excuse me.

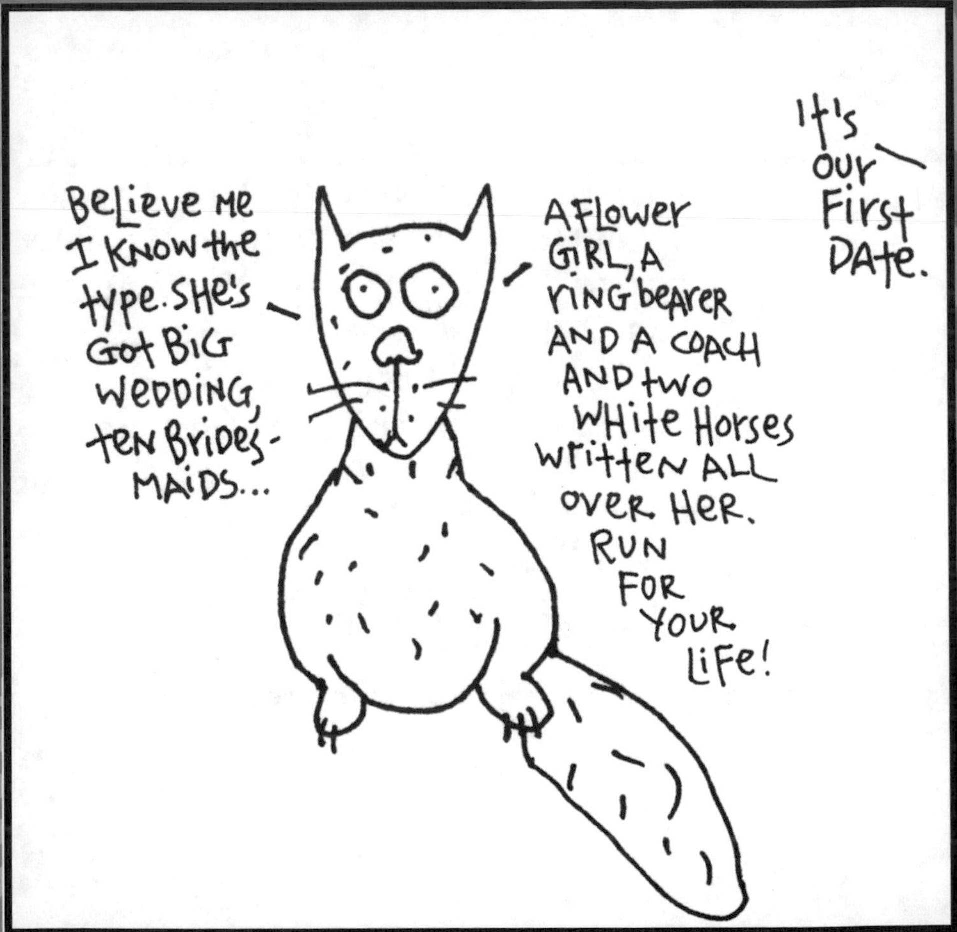
Believe me I know the type. SHE's Got BIG WEDDING, ten Brides-MAIDS...
A FLower GIRL, A ring bearer AND A COACH AND two WHite Horses written ALL over Her. RUN FOR YOUR LiFe!
It's our First DAte.

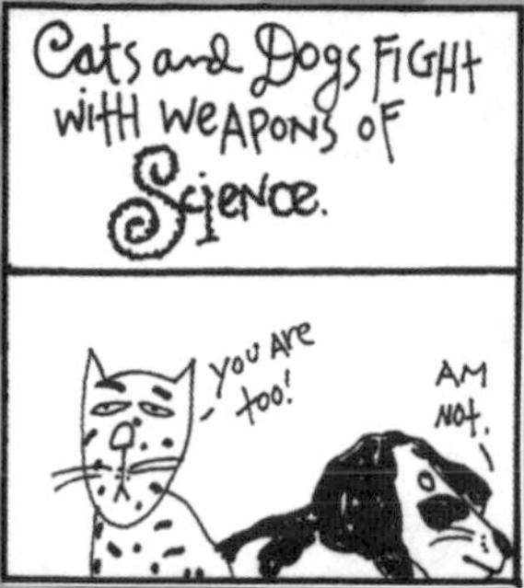
Cats and Dogs FIGHT with WEAPONS of Science.
YOU ARE too!
AM NOT.

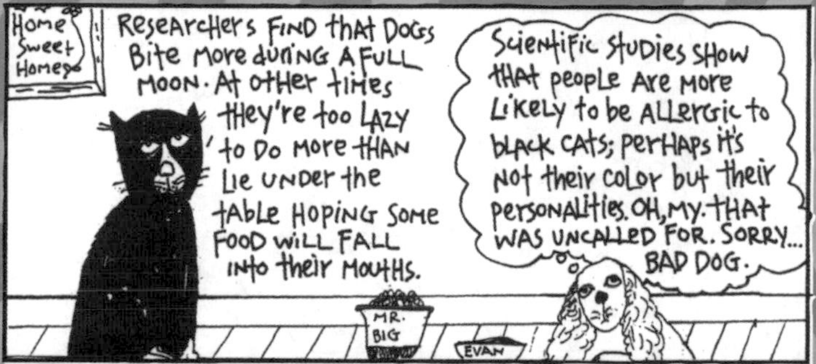
Home Sweet Home
Researchers FIND that Dogs Bite more during A FULL MOON. At other times they're too LAZY to Do more THAN Lie UNDER the table HOPING Some FOOD WILL FALL into their MOUTHS.
Scientific Studies Show THAT people Are more Likely to be ALLERGIC to black CATS; perHAPS it's not their color but their personalities. OH, MY. THAT WAS UNCALLED FOR. SORRY... BAD DOG.
MR. BIG
EVAN

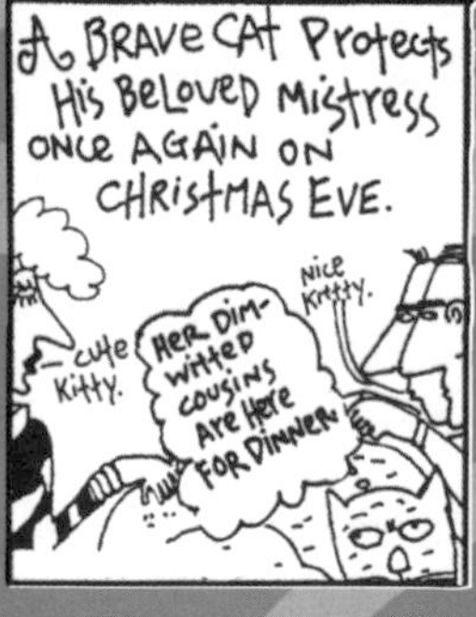
A BRAVE CAT Protects His BeLOVED Mistress ONCE AGAIN ON CHRISTMAS EVE.
Cute Kitty.
Nice Kitty.
HER DIM-WITTED COUSINS ARE HERE FOR DINNER.

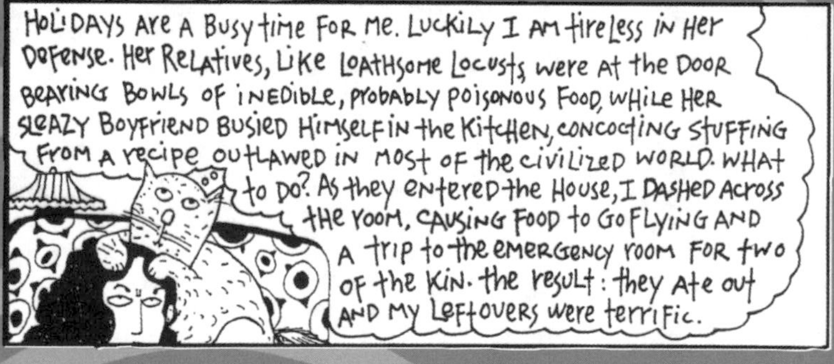
HOLIDAYS ARE A Busy time FOR ME. LUCKILY I AM tireLess IN Her DeFense. Her Relatives, Like LOATHSOME Locusts were At the DOOR bearing BOWLS OF INEDIBLE, PROBABLY POISONOUS FOOD, WHILE HER SLEAZY BOYFRIEND BUSIED HIMSELF IN the Kitchen, CONCOCTING STUFFING FROM A recipe OUTLAWED IN MOST OF the civilized WORLD. WHAT to DO? As they entered the House, I DASHED ACROSS the room, CAUSING FOOD to GO FLYING AND A trip to the emergency room FOR two of the Kin. the result: they Ate out AND MY LEFTOVERS were terrific.

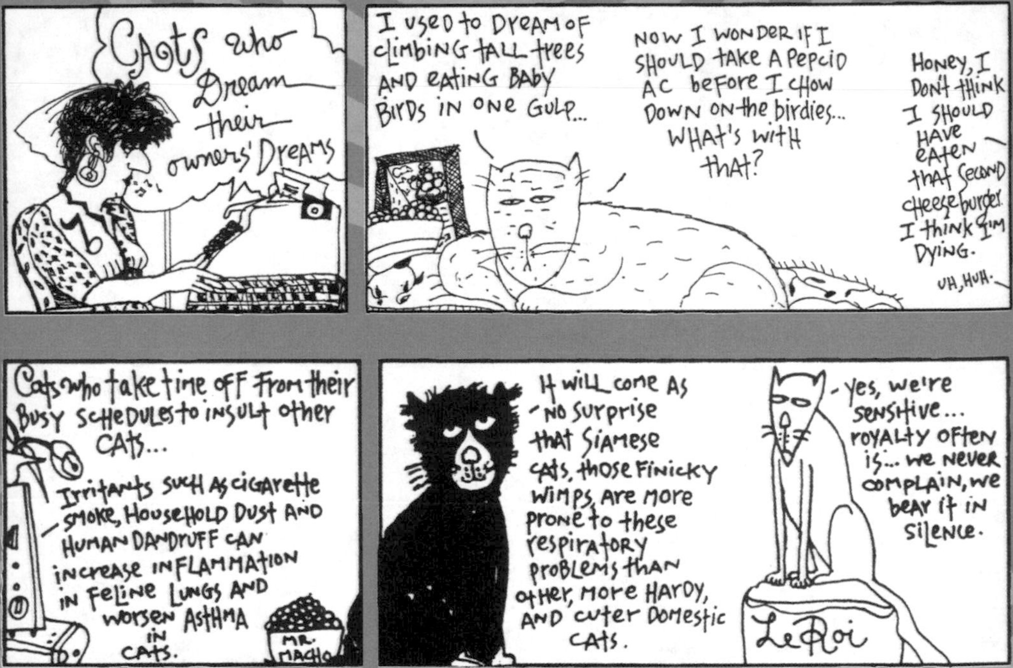
Cats who Dream their owners' Dreams
I used to dream of climbing tall trees and eating baby birds in one gulp...
Now I wonder if I should take a Pepcid AC before I chow down on the birdies... What's with that?
Honey, I don't think I should have eaten that second cheeseburger. I think I'm dying.
Uh, huh.
Cats who take time off from their busy schedules to insult other cats...
Irritants such as cigarette smoke, household dust and human dandruff can increase inflammation in feline lungs and worsen asthma in cats.
Mr. Macho
It will come as no surprise that Siamese cats, those finicky wimps, are more prone to these respiratory problems than other, more hardy, and cuter domestic cats.
Yes, we're sensitive... royalty often is... we never complain, we bear it in silence.
Le Roi

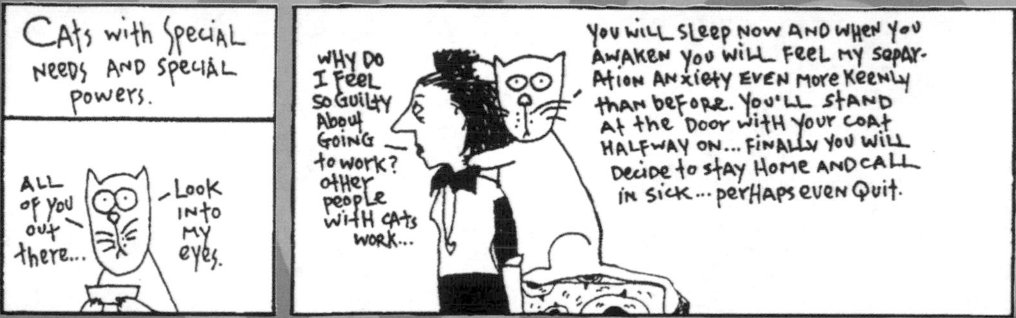
Cats with Special needs and special powers.
All of you out there...
Look into my eyes.
Why do I feel so guilty about going to work? Other people with cats work...
You will sleep now and when you awaken you will feel my separation anxiety even more keenly than before. You'll stand at the door with your coat halfway on... finally you will decide to stay home and call in sick... perhaps even quit.

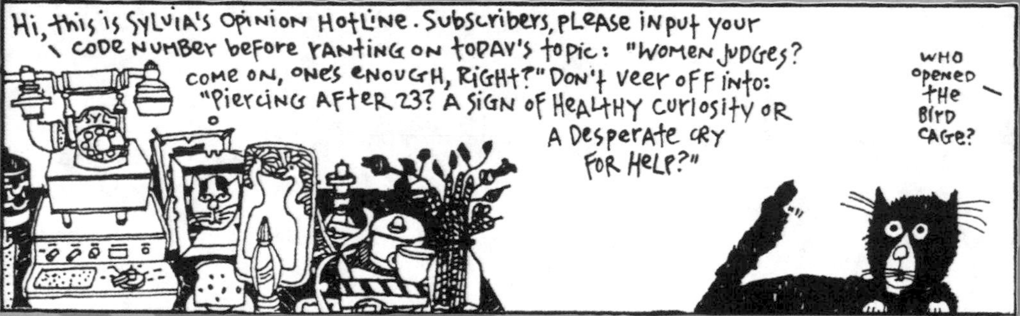
Hi, this is Sylvia's Opinion Hotline. Subscribers, please input your code number before ranting on today's topic: "Women judges? Come on, one's enough, right?" Don't veer off into: "Piercing after 23? A sign of healthy curiosity or a desperate cry for help?"
Who opened the bird cage?

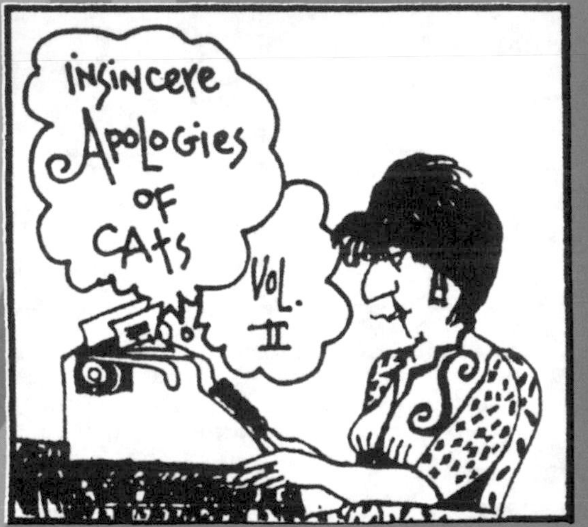
insincere Apologies of Cats
Vol. II

Rrp!
EDGAR, Get Down!
I'M SORRY...DID YOU WANT to HANG ON the DRAPES FIRST?

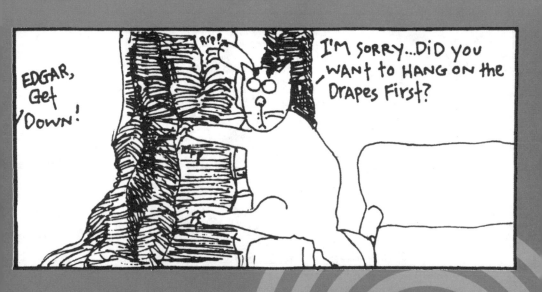

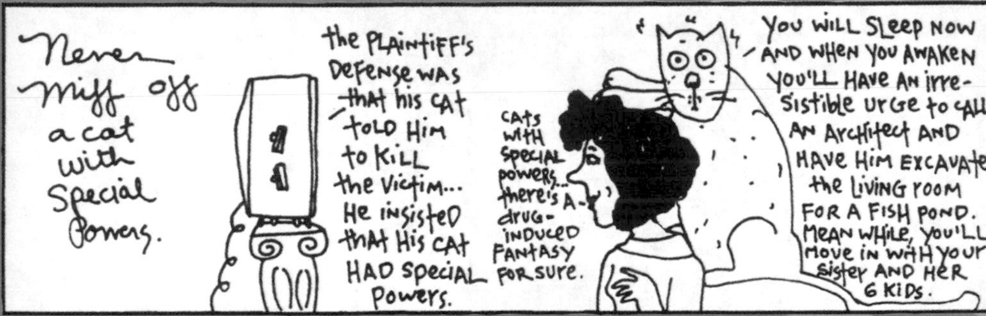
Never miff off a cat with Special Powers.
the PLAINTIFF'S DEFENSE WAS that his CAT TOLD HIM to KILL the Victim... He insisted that His CAT HAD Special Powers.
CATS WITH SPECIAL powers... there's A drug-induced FANTASY FOR sure.
YOU WILL SLeep NOW AND WHEN YOU AWAKEN YOU'LL HAVE AN irresistible urge to CALL AN Architect AND HAVE HIM EXCAVATE the LIVING room FOR A FISH POND. MEAN WHILE, YOU'LL move in with your sister AND HER 6 KIDS.

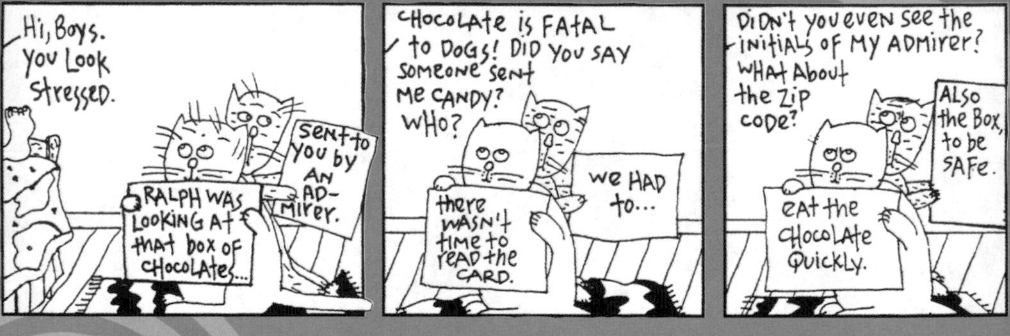
Hi, Boys. you Look stressed.
RALPH WAS LOOKING At that box of CHOCOLATes...
sent to you by AN ADMirer.
CHOCOLAte is FATAL to DOGS! DID YOU SAY SOMEONE sent ME CANDY? WHO?
there WASN'T time to read the CARD.
WE HAD to...
DIDN'T you even see the initials of MY ADMirer? WHAt About the Zip code?
eat the CHOCOLAte QUICKLY.
ALSO the Box, to be SAFe.

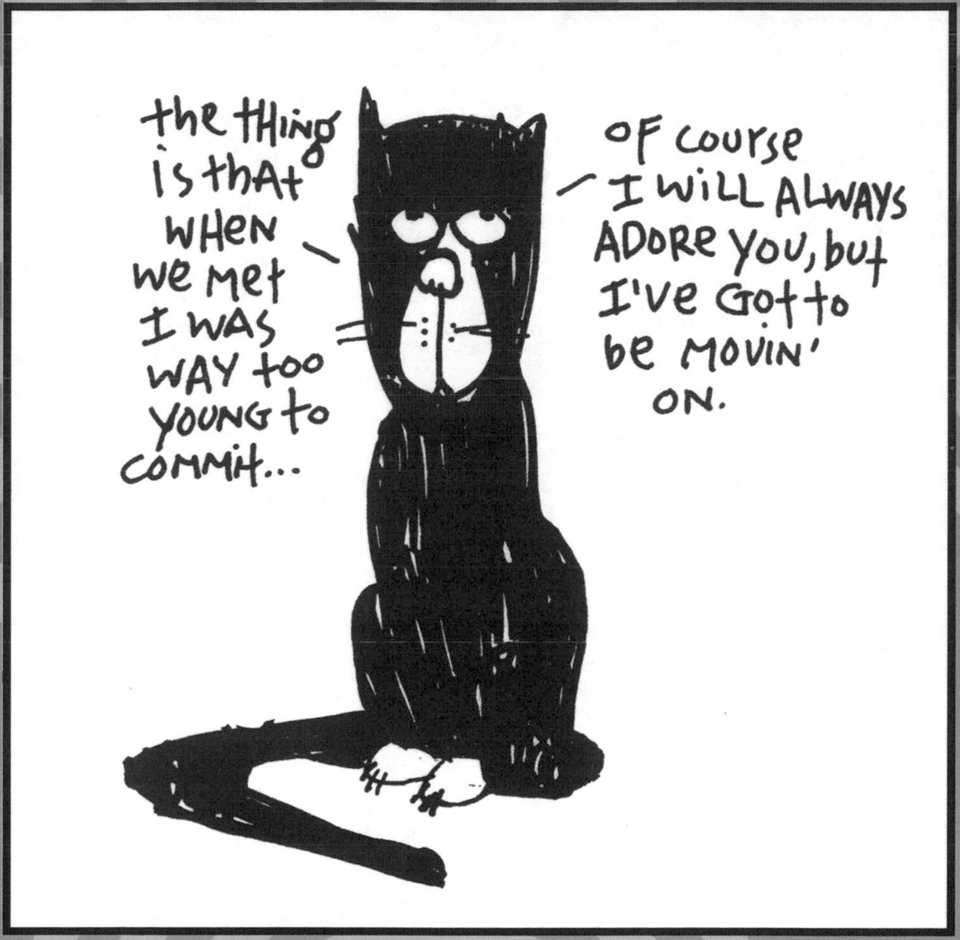
the thing is that when we met I was way too young to commit...
of course I will always adore you, but I've got to be movin' on.

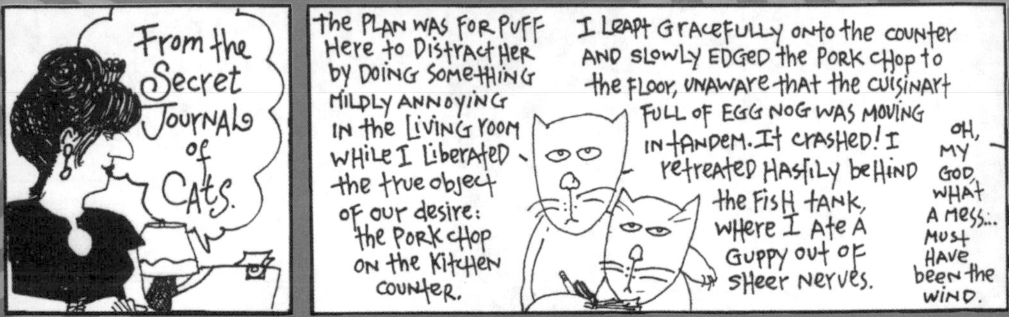
From the Secret Journal of Cats.
the PLAN WAS FOR PUFF Here to Distract Her by Doing Something Mildly Annoying in the Living room while I liberated the true object of our desire: the Pork chop on the Kitchen counter.
I Leapt Gracefully onto the counter and slowly edged the Pork chop to the floor, unaware that the cuisinart full of egg nog was moving in tandem. It crashed! I retreated hastily behind the fish tank, where I ate a guppy out of sheer nerves.
Oh, my God, what a mess... must have been the wind.

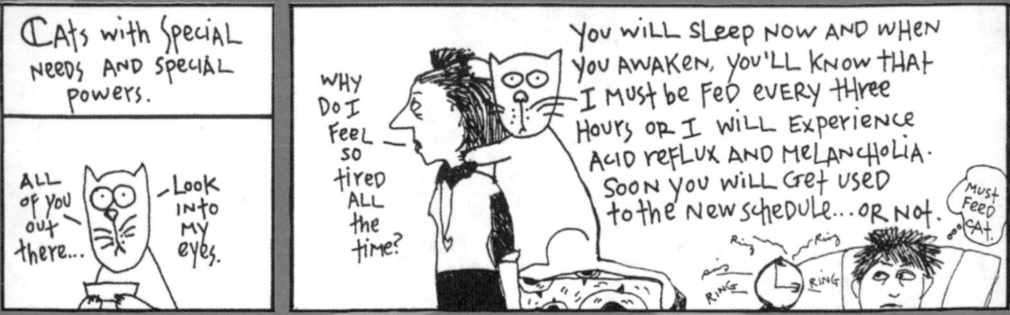
Cats with special needs and special powers.
All of you out there...
Look into my eyes.
Why do I feel so tired all the time?
You will sleep now and when you awaken, you'll know that I must be fed every three hours or I will experience acid reflux and melancholia. Soon you will get used to the new schedule... or not.
Ring
Ring
Ring
Ring
Ring
Must feed cat.

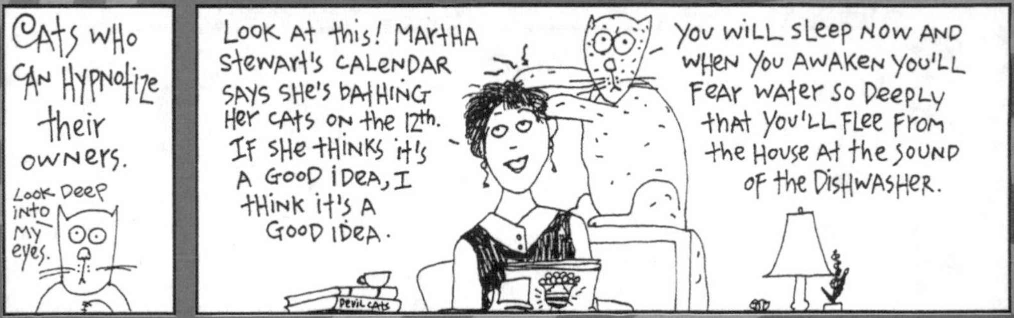
Cats who can Hypnotize their owners.
Look Deep into My eyes.
Look at this! MARTHA stewart's CALENDAR SAYS SHE'S BATHING Her cats on the 12th. IF SHe thinks it's A GOOD IDEA, I think it's A GOOD IDEA.
DEVIL CATS
You will sleep now and when you awaken you'll fear water so deeply that you'll flee from the house at the sound of the dishwasher.

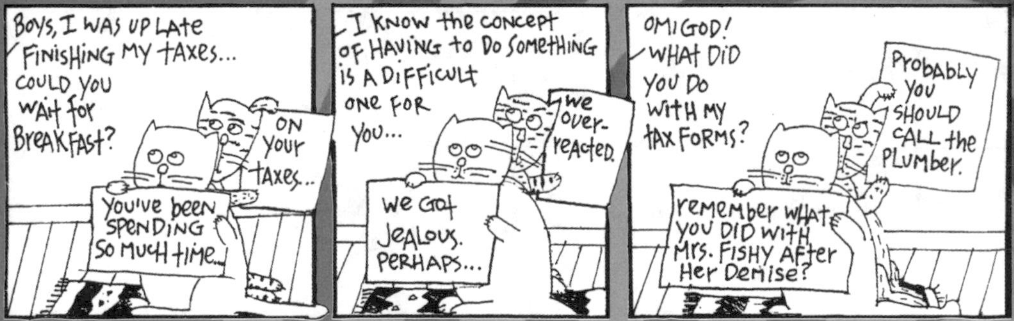
Boys, I was up late finishing my taxes... could you wait for breakfast?
You've been spending so much time...
ON your taxes...
I know the concept of having to do something is a difficult one for you...
we got jealous. perhaps...
we over-reacted.
OMIGOD! WHAT DID YOU DO WITH MY TAX FORMS?
remember what you did with Mrs. Fishy after her demise?
Probably you should call the plumber.

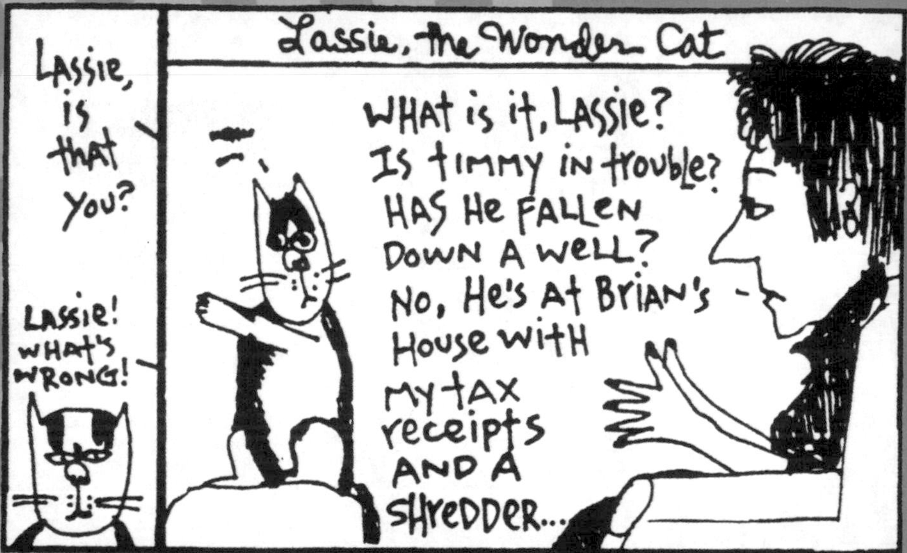
Lassie, the Wonder Cat
LASSIE, IS THAT YOU?
LASSIE! WHAT'S WRONG!
WHAT is it, LASSIE? IS timmy in trouble? HAS HE FALLEN DOWN A WELL? No, He's At BRIAN's House with my tax receipts AND A SHREDDER...

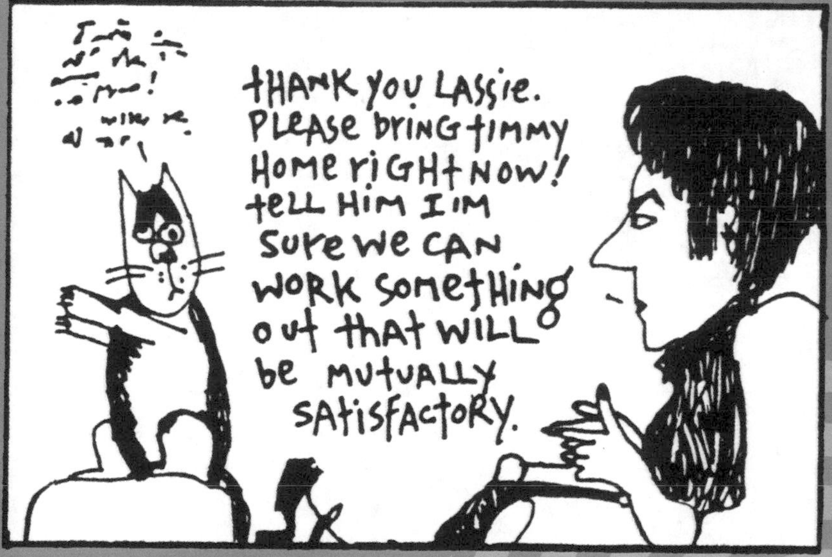
THANK YOU LASSIE. PLEASE BRING TIMMY HOME RIGHT NOW! TELL HIM I'M SURE WE CAN WORK SOMETHING OUT THAT WILL BE MUTUALLY SATISFACTORY.

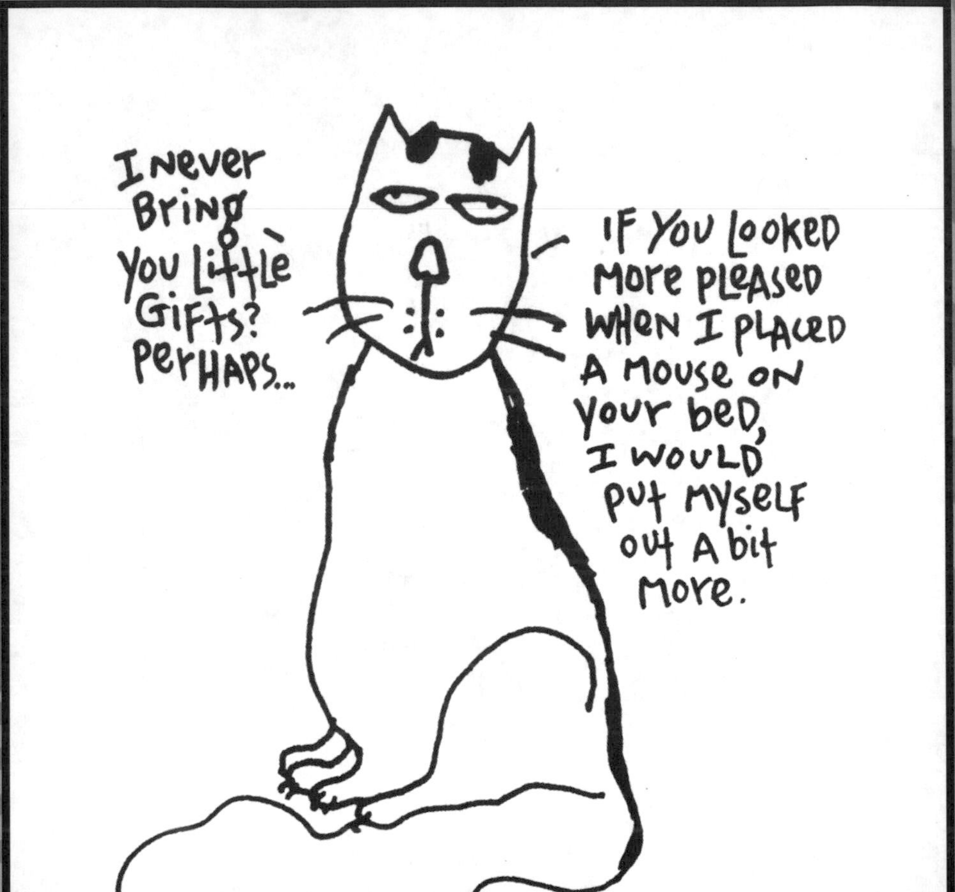
I Never Bring you Little Gifts? PerHAPS...
IF YOU LOOKED MORE PLEASED WHEN I PLACED A MOUSE ON YOUR BED, I WOULD PUT MYSELF OUT A BIT MORE.

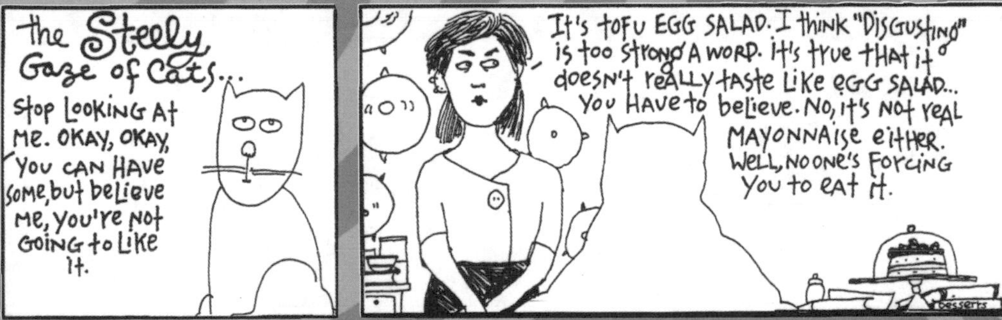
the Steely Gaze of Cats...
Stop Looking At me. OKAY, OKAY, You CAN HAVE some, but believe me, you're not going to like it.
It's tofu EGG SALAD. I think "Disgusting" is too strong a word. It's true that it doesn't really taste like egg salad... You have to believe. No, it's not real mayonnaise either. Well, no one's forcing you to eat it.

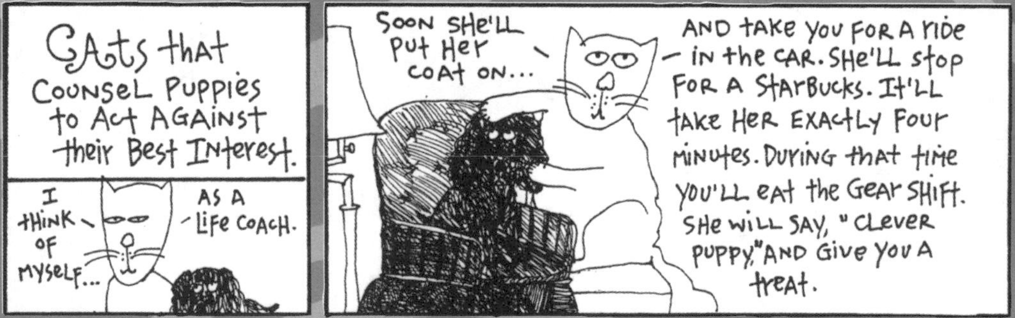
Cats that Counsel Puppies to Act Against their Best Interest.
I think of myself...
As a Life Coach.
Soon she'll put her coat on...
And take you for a ride in the car. She'll stop for a Starbucks. It'll take her exactly four minutes. During that time you'll eat the gear shift. She will say, "Clever puppy," and give you a treat.

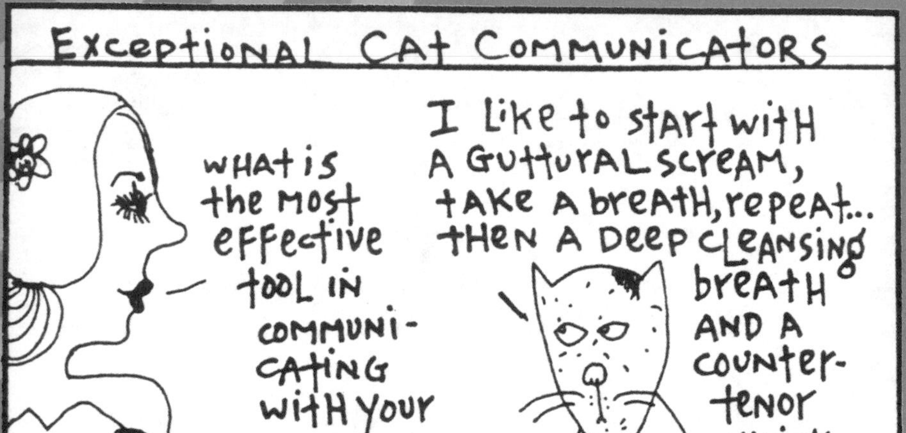
Exceptional Cat Communicators
what is the most effective tool in communicating with your human companions?
I like to start with a guttural scream, take a breath, repeat... then a deep cleansing breath and a counter-tenor shriek.

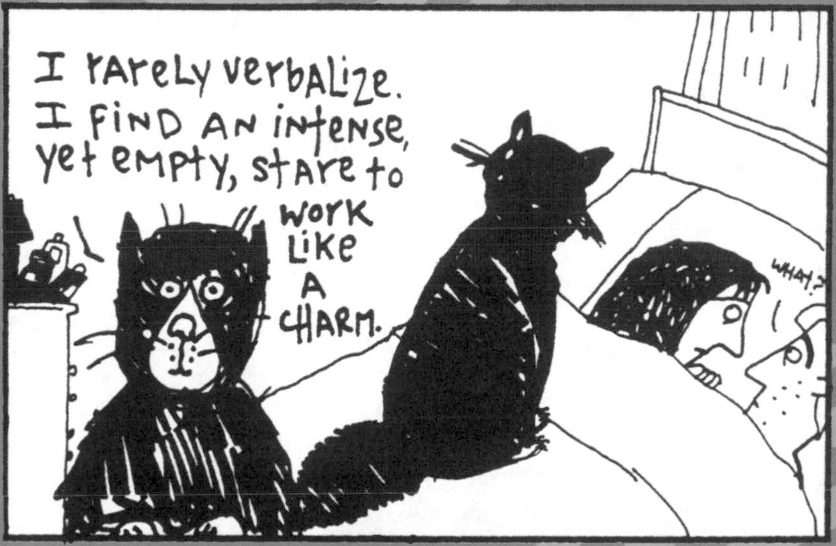
I rarely verbalize. I find an intense, yet empty, stare to work like a charm.
WHAT?

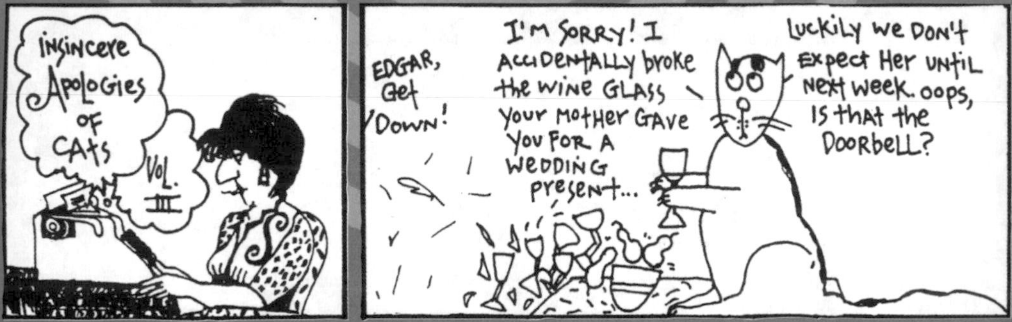
insincere Apologies of Cats
Vol. III
EDGAR, Get Down!
I'M SORRY! I ACCIDENTALLY broke the WINE GLASS your Mother GAVE YOU FOR A WEDDING present...
Luckily we DON'T expect Her until next week. oops, is that the Doorbell?

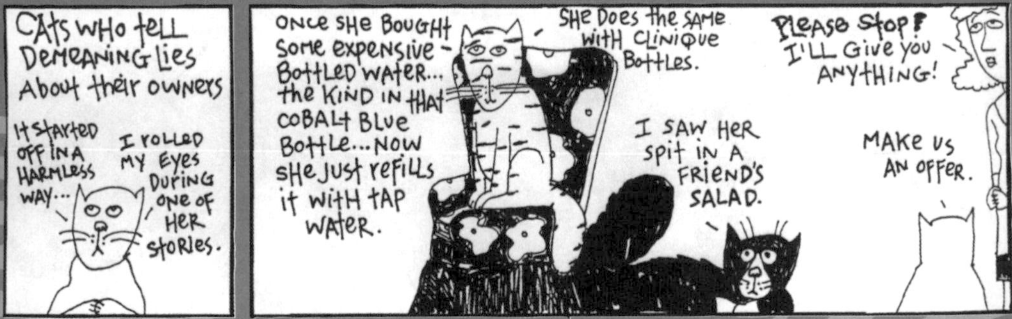
CATS WHO tell Demeaning Lies About their owners
It started off in a harmless way...
I rolled my eyes during one of her stories.
ONCE SHE BOUGHT some expensive Bottled water... the KIND IN THAT COBALT BLUE Bottle... NOW SHE JUST refills it with tap water.
SHE Does the same with Clinique Bottles.
I SAW HER spit in a friend's salad.
Please Stop! I'LL Give you ANYTHING!
MAKE US AN OFFER.

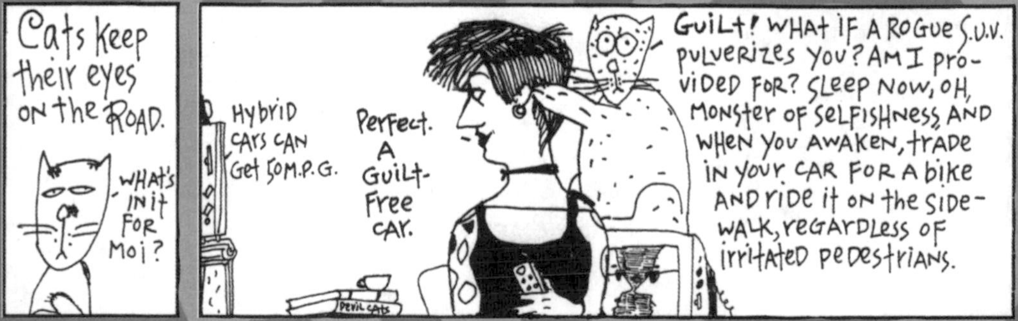
Cats keep their eyes on the ROAD.
WHAT's IN it FOR Moi?
Hybrid CARS CAN Get 50 M.P.G.
Perfect. A Guilt-Free CAR.
GUILT! WHAT IF A ROGUE S.U.V. PULVERIZES YOU? AM I PROVIDED FOR? SLEEP NOW, OH, MONSTER OF SELFISHNESS, AND WHEN YOU AWAKEN, TRADE IN YOUR CAR FOR A BIKE AND RIDE IT ON THE SIDEWALK, REGARDLESS OF IRRITATED PEDESTRIANS.
DEVIL CATS

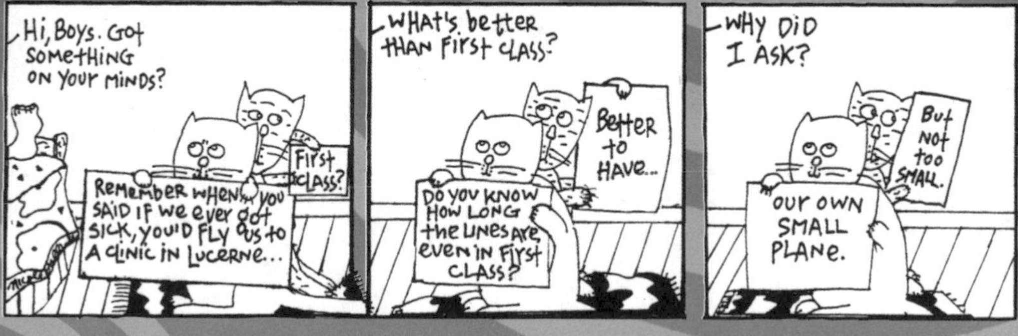
Hi, Boys. Got something on your minds?
Remember when you said if we ever got sick, you'd fly us to a clinic in Lucerne...
First class?
WHAT's better than First class?
Do you know how long the lines are, even in First class?
Better to have...
WHY DID I ASK?
Our own small plane.
But not too small.

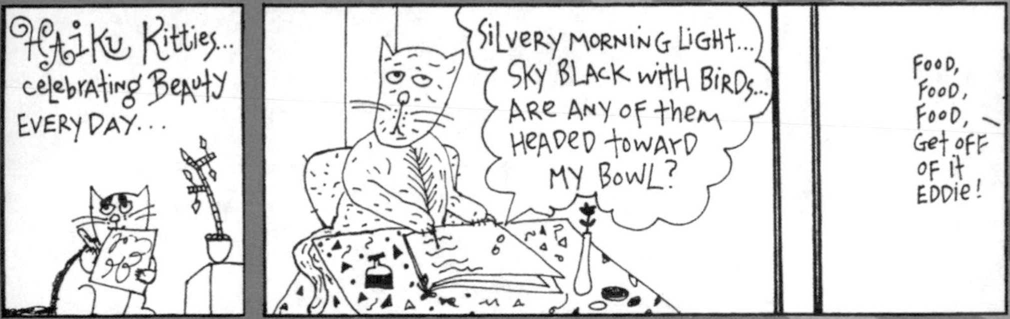
Haiku Kitties...
celebrating Beauty
EVERY DAY...
SiLVERY MORNING LIGHT...
SKY BLACK with BIRDS...
ARE ANY OF them
HEADED toWARD
MY BOWL?
FOOD,
FOOD,
FOOD,
Get off
of it
EDDIE!

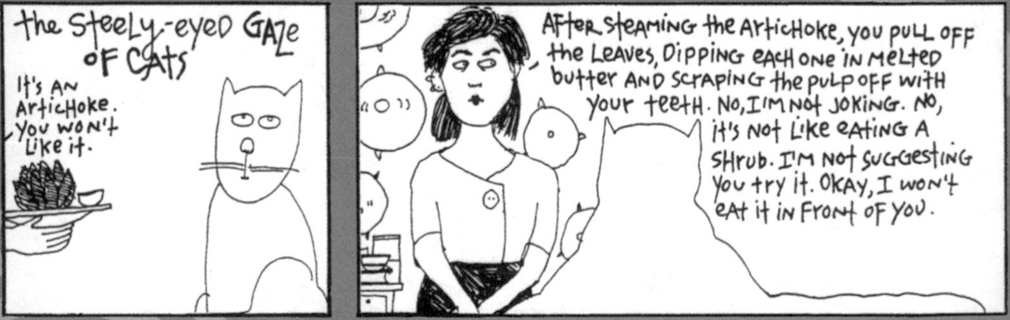
the Steely-eyed GAZE
OF CATS
It's AN
ArtichoKe.
You WON't
Like it.
After steaming the Artichoke, you pull off the Leaves, Dipping each one in melted butter and scraping the pulp off with your teeth. No, I'm not joking. No, it's not like eating a shrub. I'm not suggesting you try it. Okay, I won't eat it in front of you.

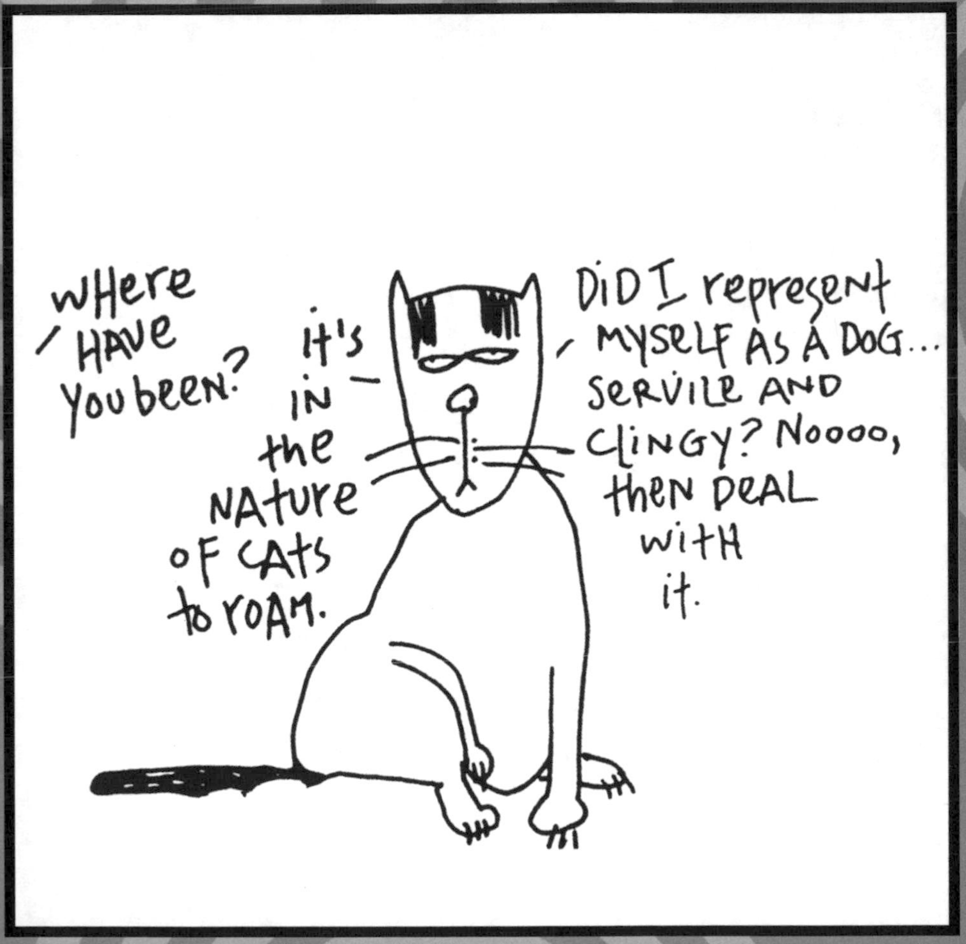

wHere HAVe you been?
it's in the NAture of cAts to roAM.
DiD I represent MYSeLF AS A DoG... SeRViLe AND CLiNGY? Noooo, then DeAL with it.

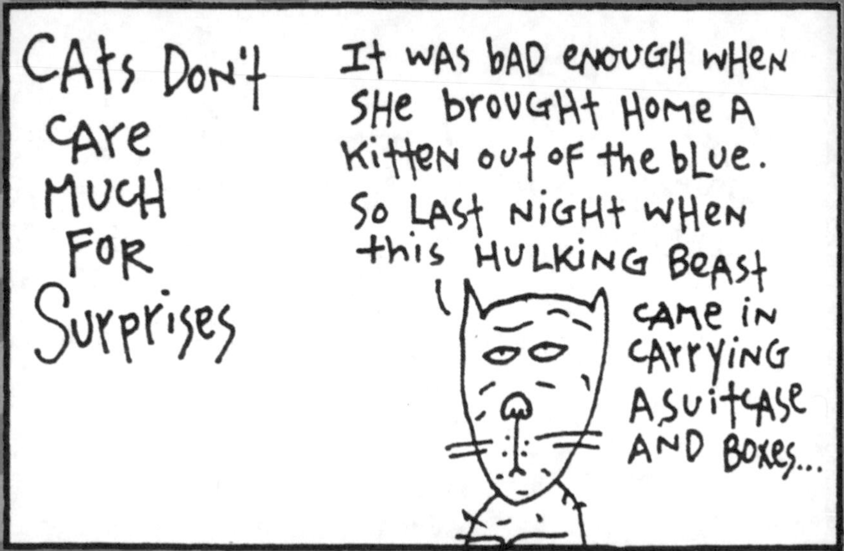
CAts Don't CAre MUCH FOR Surprises
It WAS bAD eNOUGH WHeN SHe brOUGHt HOme A Kitten out of the bLue.
So LAST NIGHt WHeN this HULKiNG BeASt
CAme iN CArryiNG A SuitCASe AND Boxes...

I WAS ENRAGED.
SHE SAID, "HE LOVES
CATS." UH, HUH...

THEN THE NEW KITTEN
WALKED OVER TO HIS
SUITCASE AND DID
SOMETHING UNCOUTH.
BRAVO! I MIGHT GROW
FOND OF HER.

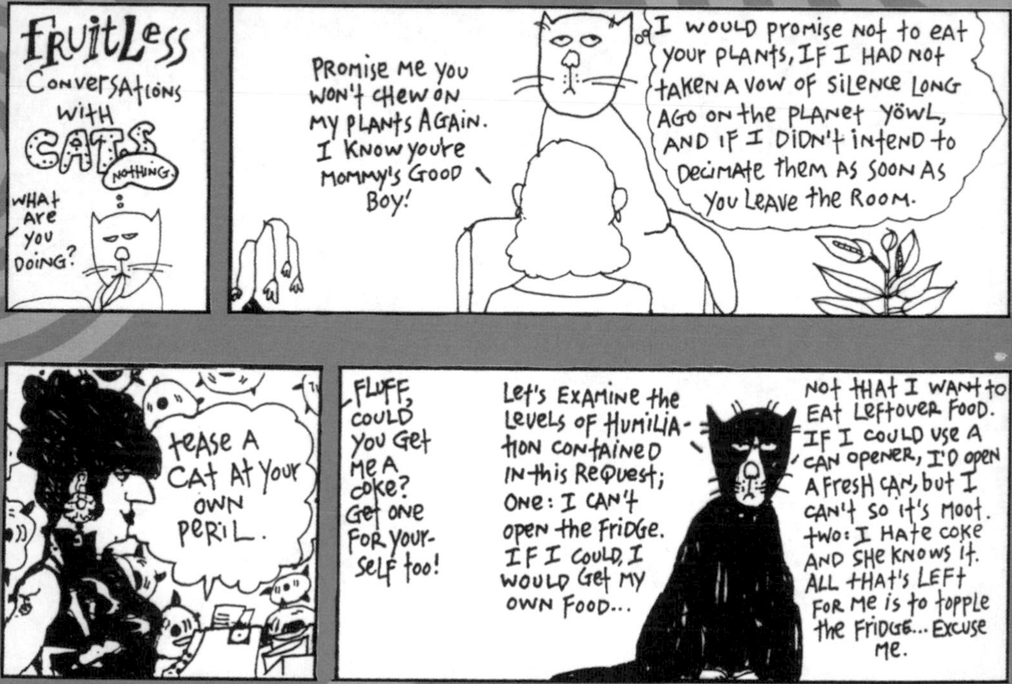
FRUITLESS
CONVERSATIONS WITH
CATS
WHAT ARE YOU DOING?
NOTHING.
PROMISE ME YOU WON'T CHEW ON MY PLANTS AGAIN. I KNOW YOU'RE MOMMY'S GOOD BOY!
I WOULD PROMISE NOT TO EAT YOUR PLANTS, IF I HAD NOT TAKEN A VOW OF SILENCE LONG AGO ON THE PLANET YÖWL, AND IF I DIDN'T INTEND TO DECIMATE THEM AS SOON AS YOU LEAVE THE ROOM.
TEASE A CAT AT YOUR OWN PERIL.
FLUFF, COULD YOU GET ME A COKE? GET ONE FOR YOURSELF TOO!
LET'S EXAMINE THE LEVELS OF HUMILIATION CONTAINED IN THIS REQUEST; ONE: I CAN'T OPEN THE FRIDGE. IF I COULD, I WOULD GET MY OWN FOOD...
NOT THAT I WANT TO EAT LEFTOVER FOOD. IF I COULD USE A CAN OPENER, I'D OPEN A FRESH CAN, BUT I CAN'T SO IT'S MOOT. TWO: I HATE COKE AND SHE KNOWS IT. ALL THAT'S LEFT FOR ME IS TO TOPPLE THE FRIDGE... EXCUSE ME.

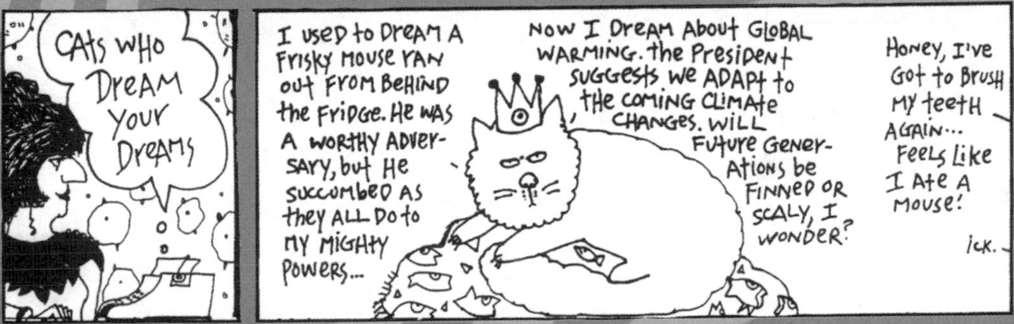
Cats who dream your dreams
I used to dream a frisky mouse ran out from behind the fridge. He was a worthy adversary, but he succumbed as they all do to my mighty powers...
Now I dream about global warming. the President suggests we adapt to the coming climate changes. Will future generations be finned or scaly, I wonder?
Honey, I've got to brush my teeth again... Feels like I ate a mouse!
ick.

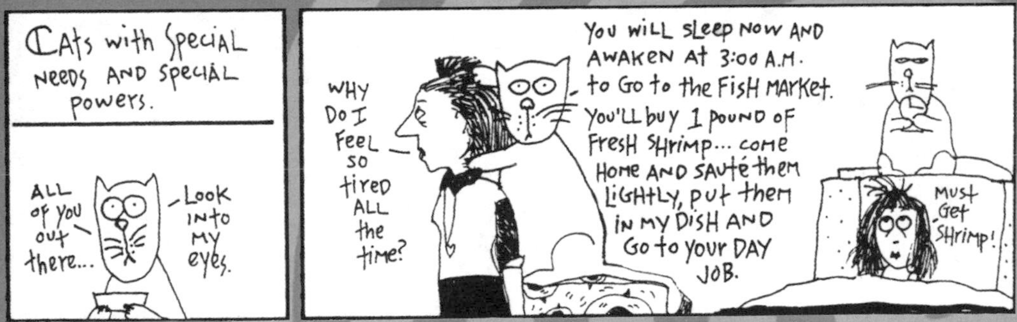
Cats with special needs and special powers.
All of you out there...
Look into my eyes.
Why do I feel so tired all the time?
You will sleep now and awaken at 3:00 A.M. to go to the fish market. You'll buy 1 pound of fresh shrimp... come home and sauté them lightly, put them in my dish and go to your day job.
Must get shrimp!

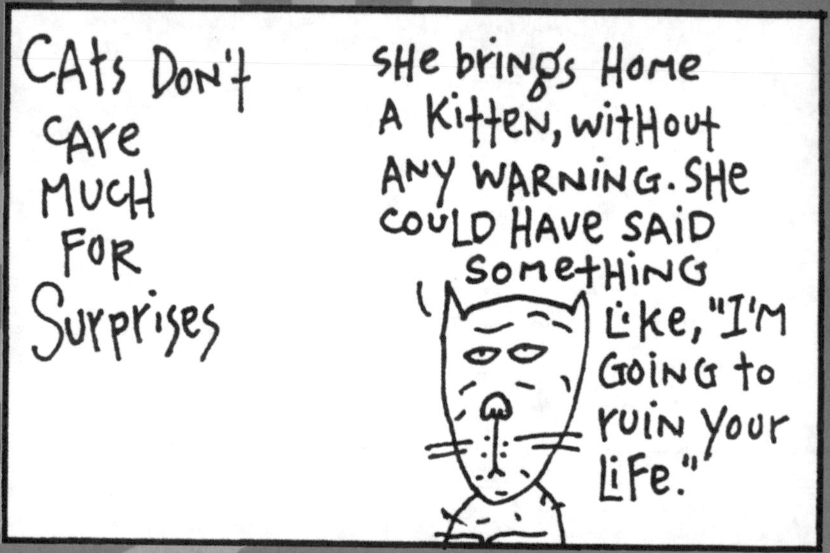
CAts Don't care much for Surprises
SHe brings Home A Kitten, withOut ANY WARNING. SHe COULD HAVE SAID something Like, "I'M GOING to ruin your Life."

But no, she just brings the thing in and says, "Isn't she adorable?"

I say, "If the children from 'the Village of the Damned' had kittens, she'd be the pick of the litter."

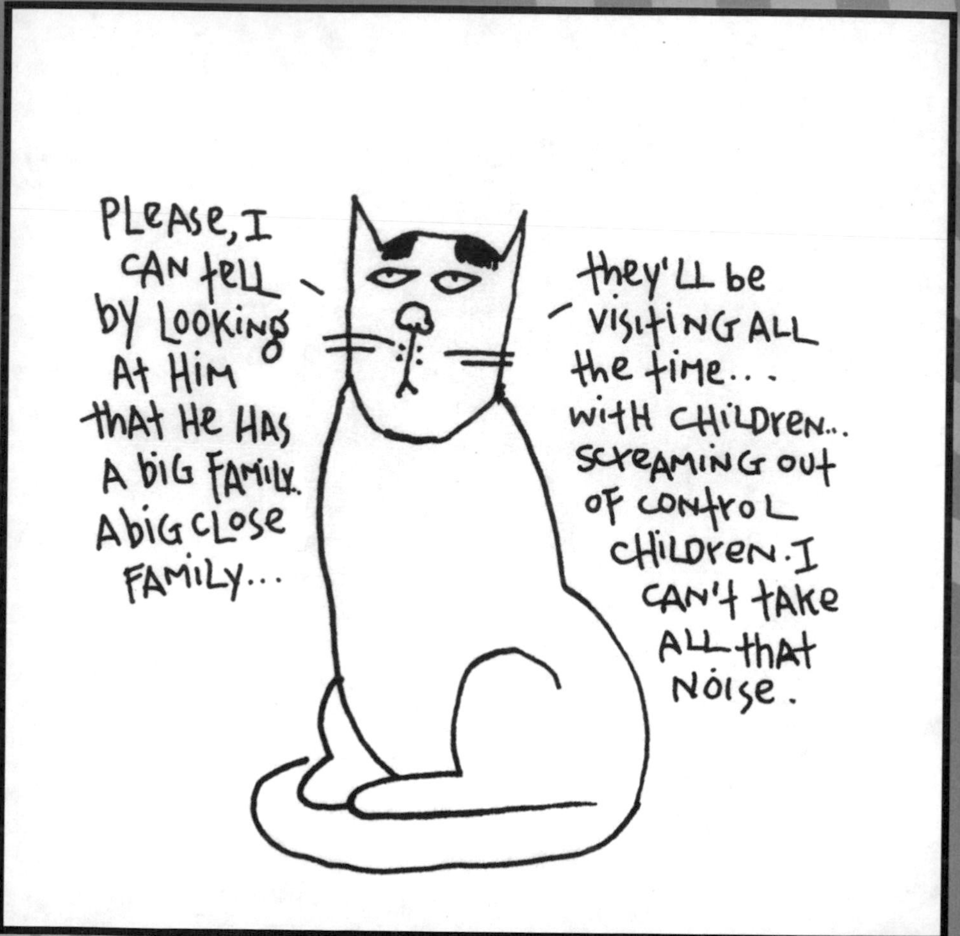
PLEASE, I CAN TELL BY LOOKING AT HIM THAT HE HAS A BIG FAMILY.. A BIG CLOSE FAMILY...
THEY'LL BE VISITING ALL THE TIME... WITH CHILDREN... SCREAMING OUT OF CONTROL CHILDREN. I CAN'T TAKE ALL THAT NOISE.

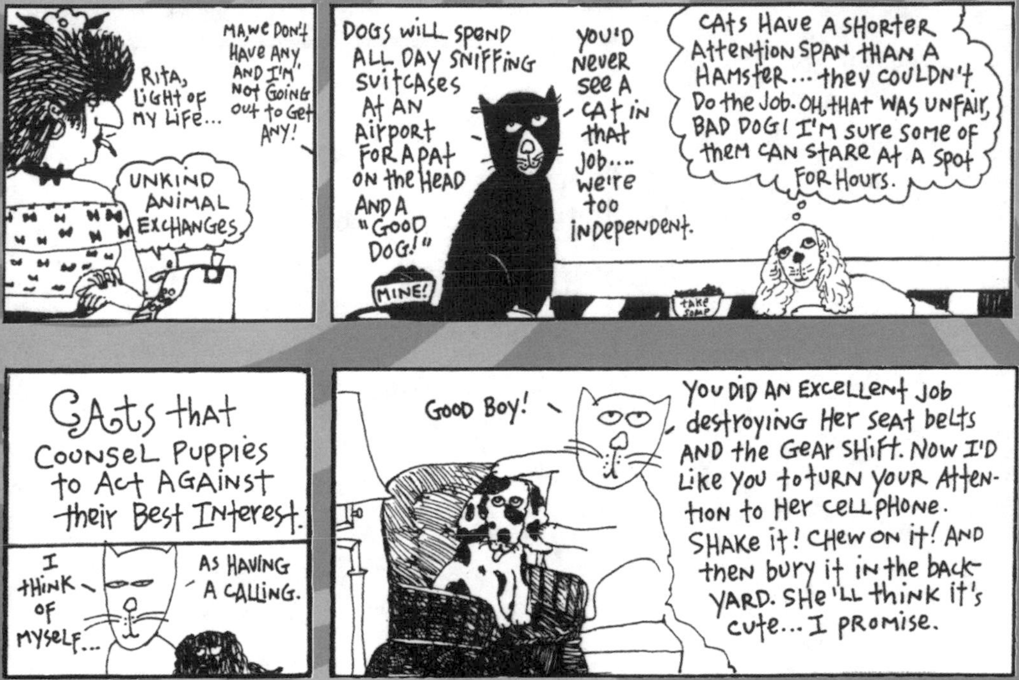
RITA, LIGHT OF MY LIFE...
MA, WE DON'T HAVE ANY, AND I'M NOT GOING OUT TO GET ANY!
UNKIND ANIMAL EXCHANGES
DOGS WILL SPEND ALL DAY SNIFFING SUITCASES AT AN AIRPORT FOR A PAT ON THE HEAD AND A "GOOD DOG!"
YOU'D NEVER SEE A CAT IN THAT JOB.... WE'RE TOO INDEPENDENT.
CATS HAVE A SHORTER ATTENTION SPAN THAN A HAMSTER... THEY COULDN'T DO THE JOB. OH, THAT WAS UNFAIR, BAD DOG! I'M SURE SOME OF THEM CAN STARE AT A SPOT FOR HOURS.
MINE!
CATS THAT COUNSEL PUPPIES TO ACT AGAINST THEIR BEST INTEREST.
I THINK OF MYSELF...
AS HAVING A CALLING.
GOOD BOY!
YOU DID AN EXCELLENT JOB DESTROYING HER SEAT BELTS AND THE GEAR SHIFT. NOW I'D LIKE YOU TO TURN YOUR ATTENTION TO HER CELLPHONE. SHAKE IT! CHEW ON IT! AND THEN BURY IT IN THE BACKYARD. SHE'LL THINK IT'S CUTE... I PROMISE.

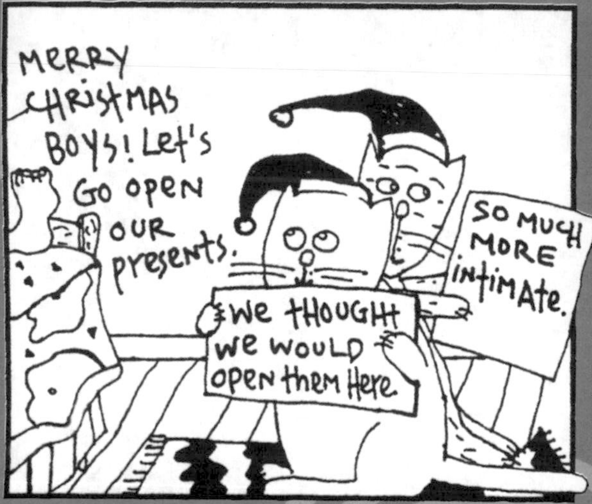

MERRY CHRISTMAS BOYS! LET'S GO OPEN OUR PRESENTS.
WE THOUGHT WE WOULD OPEN THEM HERE.
SO MUCH MORE INTIMATE.

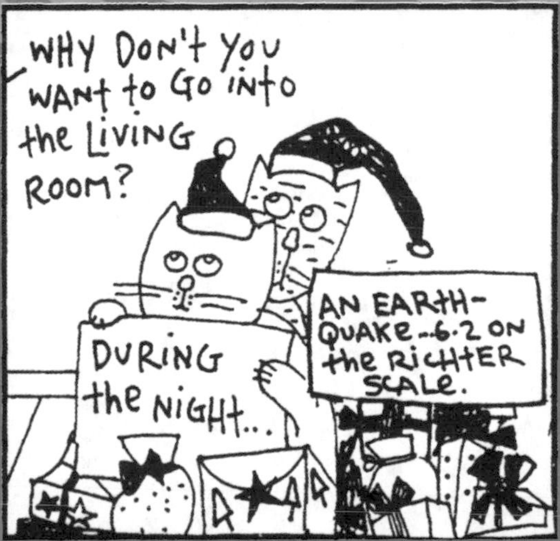
WHY DON'T YOU WANT TO GO INTO THE LIVING ROOM?
DURING THE NIGHT...
AN EARTH-QUAKE...6.2 ON THE RICHTER SCALE.

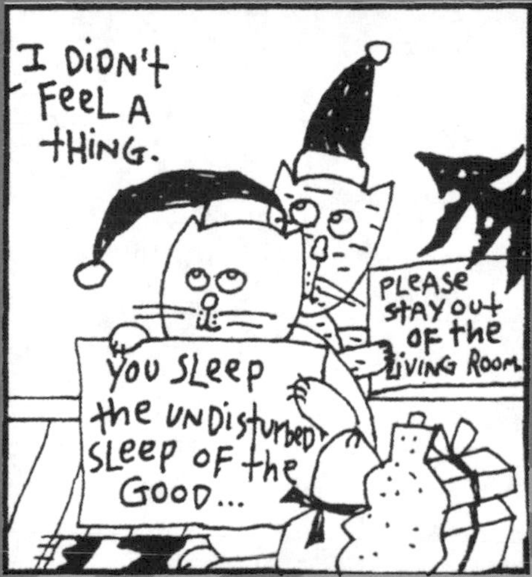
I DIDN'T FEEL A THING.
YOU SLEEP THE UNDISTURBED SLEEP OF THE GOOD...
PLEASE STAY OUT OF THE LIVING ROOM

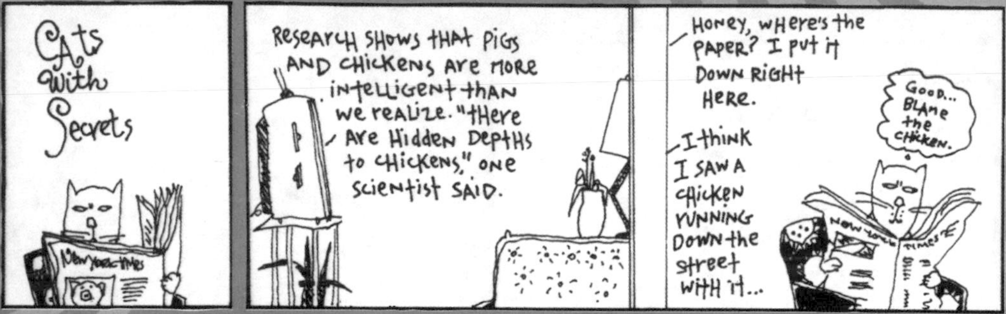
Cats with Secrets
Research shows that pigs and chickens are more intelligent than we realize. "There are hidden depths to chickens," one scientist said.
Honey, where's the paper? I put it down right here.
I think I saw a chicken running down the street with it...
Good... Blame the chicken.

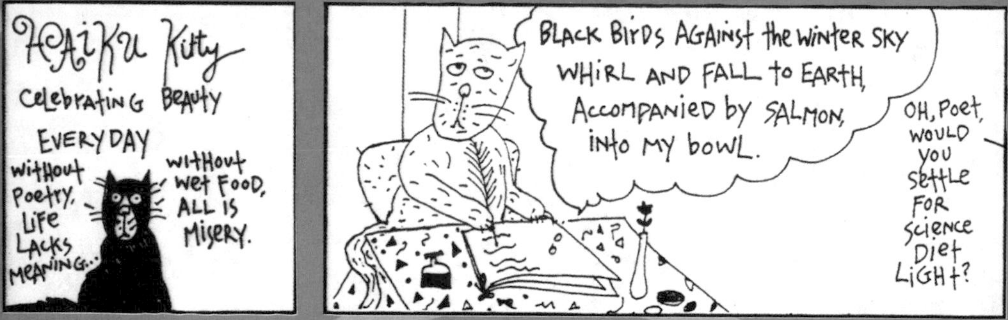
Haiku Kitty
Celebrating beauty everyday
Without poetry, life lacks meaning...
Without wet food, all is misery.
Black birds against the winter sky
whirl and fall to earth,
accompanied by salmon,
into my bowl.
Oh, poet, would you settle for Science Diet Light?

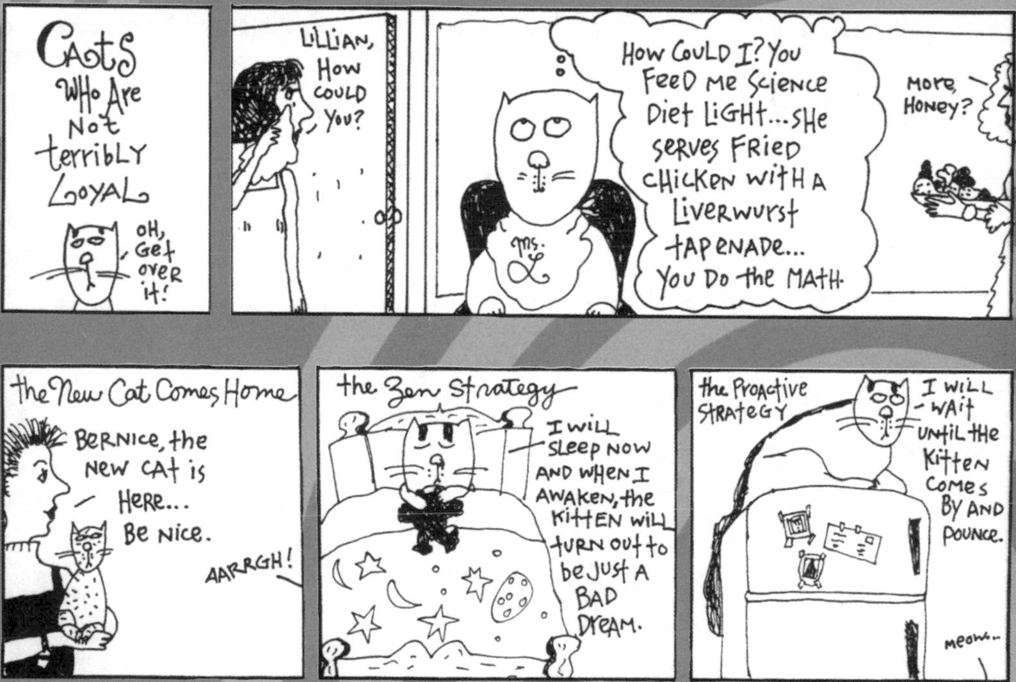
Cats Who Are Not terribly Loyal
OH, Get over it!
LILLIAN, How COULD You?
How COULD I? You Feed me Science Diet LIGHT... SHe serves FRIED CHICKEN WITH A Liverwurst tapenade... You Do the MATH.
More, Honey?
Ms. L
the New Cat Comes Home
BERNICE, the new CAT is HERE... Be nice.
AARRGH!
the Zen Strategy
I WILL SLEEP NOW AND WHEN I AWAKEN, the KITTEN WILL TURN OUT to be JUST A BAD DREAM.
the Proactive STRATEGY
I WILL WAIT UNTIL the Kitten Comes BY AND POUNCE.
meow...

the New England JOURNAL OF CATS
HARVEY, DID YOU see this?!
CATS GETTING BIG!
FIGURE 1
NORMAL CATS

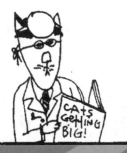

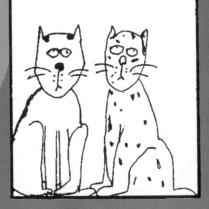

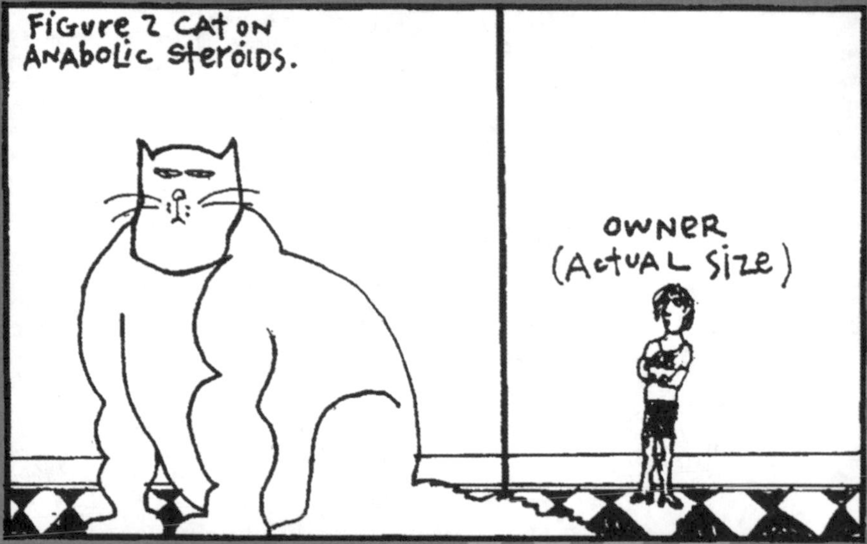
Figure 2 CAT ON ANABOLIC STEROIDS.
OWNER (ACTUAL SIZE)

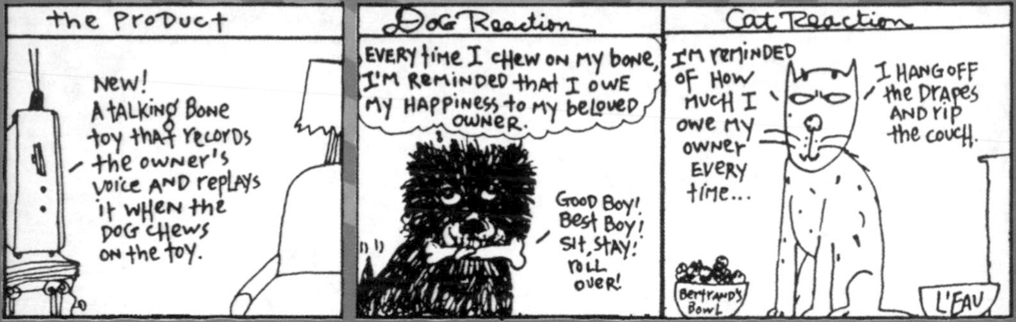
the Product
New! A talking Bone toy that records the owner's voice and replays it when the dog chews on the toy.
Dog Reaction
EVERY time I chew on my bone, I'M REMINDED that I OWE MY HAPPINESS to MY beloved OWNER.
GOOD BOY! Best Boy! Sit, STAY! roll over!
Cat Reaction
I'M reminded of how much I owe my owner every time...
I HANG OFF the Drapes AND rip the couch.
Bertrand's Bowl
L'EAU

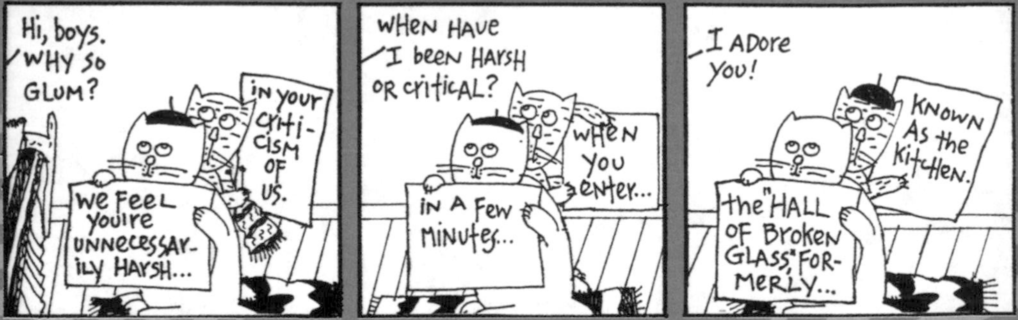
Hi, boys. WHY SO GLUM?
We feel you're unnecessarily harsh...
in your criticism of us.
WHEN HAVE I been HARSH OR critical?
in a few minutes...
when you enter...
I ADORE you!
the "HALL of Broken Glass," formerly...
known as the kitchen.

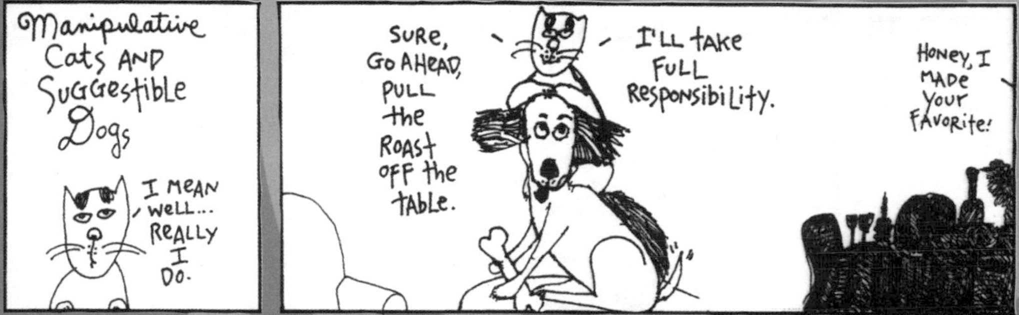
Manipulative Cats AND Suggestible Dogs
I MEAN WELL... REALLY I DO.
SURE, GO AHEAD, PULL the ROAST OFF the TABLE.
I'LL take FULL Responsibility.
Honey, I MADE your FAVORite!

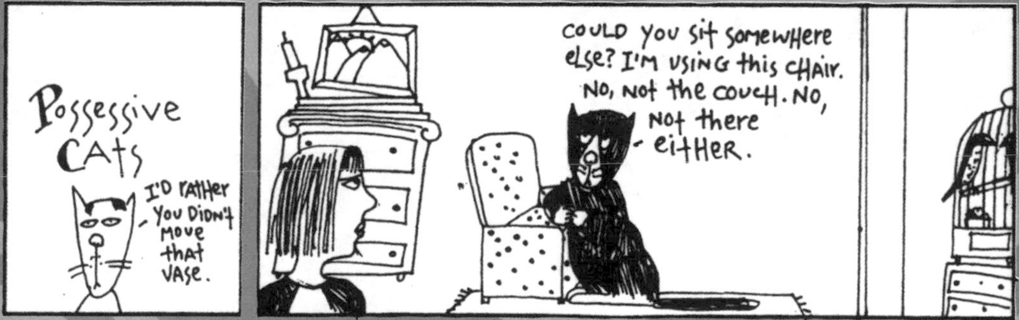
Possessive CATs
I'D rather You DIDN'T MOVE that VASE.
COULD you sit somewhere else? I'M USING this CHAIR. No, Not the couCH. No, Not there either.

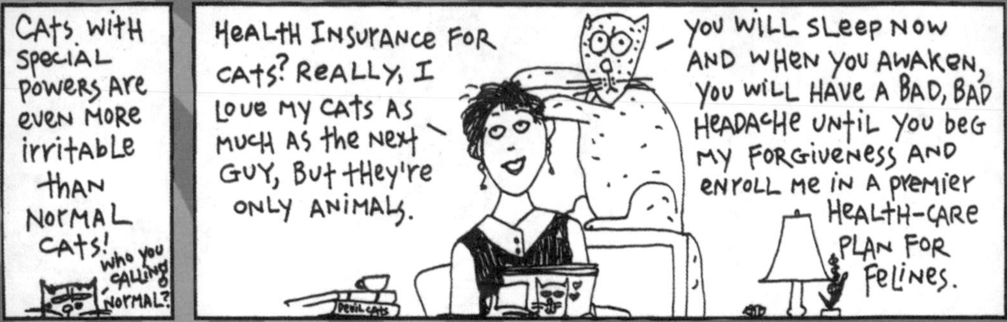
CATS WITH SPECIAL POWERS ARE EVEN MORE IRRITABLE THAN NORMAL CATS!
WHO YOU CALLING NORMAL?
HEALTH INSURANCE FOR CATS? REALLY, I LOVE MY CATS AS MUCH AS THE NEXT GUY, BUT THEY'RE ONLY ANIMALS.
YOU WILL SLEEP NOW AND WHEN YOU AWAKEN, YOU WILL HAVE A BAD, BAD HEADACHE UNTIL YOU BEG MY FORGIVENESS AND ENROLL ME IN A PREMIER HEALTH-CARE PLAN FOR FELINES.

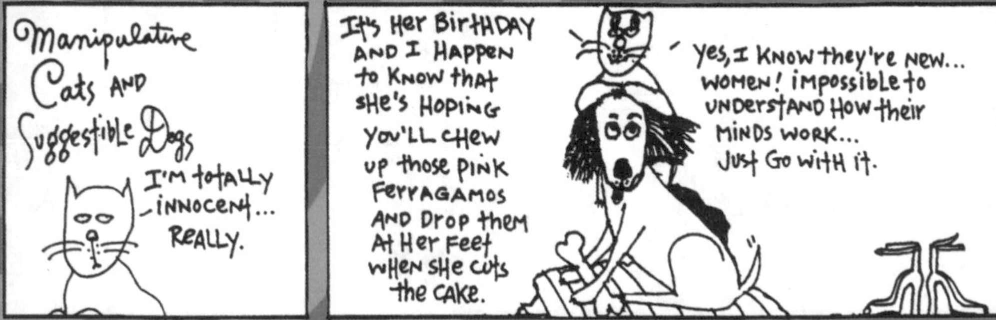
Manipulative Cats AND Suggestible Dogs
I'M TOTALLY INNOCENT... REALLY.
IT'S HER BIRTHDAY AND I HAPPEN TO KNOW THAT SHE'S HOPING YOU'LL CHEW UP THOSE PINK FERRAGAMOS AND DROP THEM AT HER FEET WHEN SHE CUTS THE CAKE.
YES, I KNOW THEY'RE NEW... WOMEN! IMPOSSIBLE TO UNDERSTAND HOW THEIR MINDS WORK... JUST GO WITH IT.

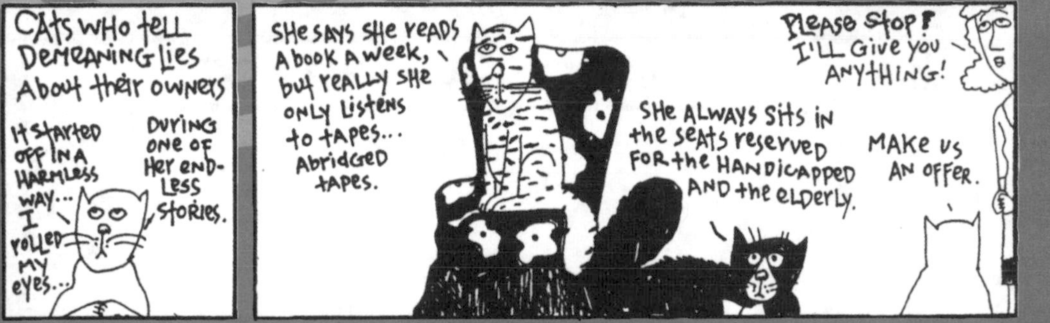
CATS WHO TELL DEMEANING LIES ABOUT THEIR OWNERS
IT STARTED OFF IN A HARMLESS WAY... I ROLLED MY EYES...
DURING ONE OF HER ENDLESS STORIES.
SHE SAYS SHE READS A BOOK A WEEK, BUT REALLY SHE ONLY LISTENS TO TAPES... ABRIDGED TAPES.
SHE ALWAYS SITS IN THE SEATS RESERVED FOR THE HANDICAPPED AND THE ELDERLY.
PLEASE STOP! I'LL GIVE YOU ANYTHING!
MAKE US AN OFFER.

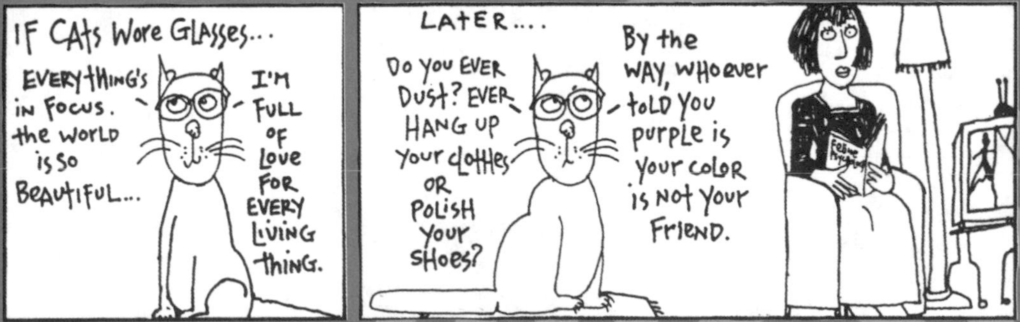
IF CATS WORE GLASSES...
EVERYTHING'S IN FOCUS. THE WORLD IS SO BEAUTIFUL...
I'M FULL OF LOVE FOR EVERY LIVING THING.
LATER....
DO YOU EVER DUST? EVER HANG UP YOUR CLOTHES OR POLISH YOUR SHOES?
BY THE WAY, WHOEVER TOLD YOU PURPLE IS YOUR COLOR IS NOT YOUR FRIEND.

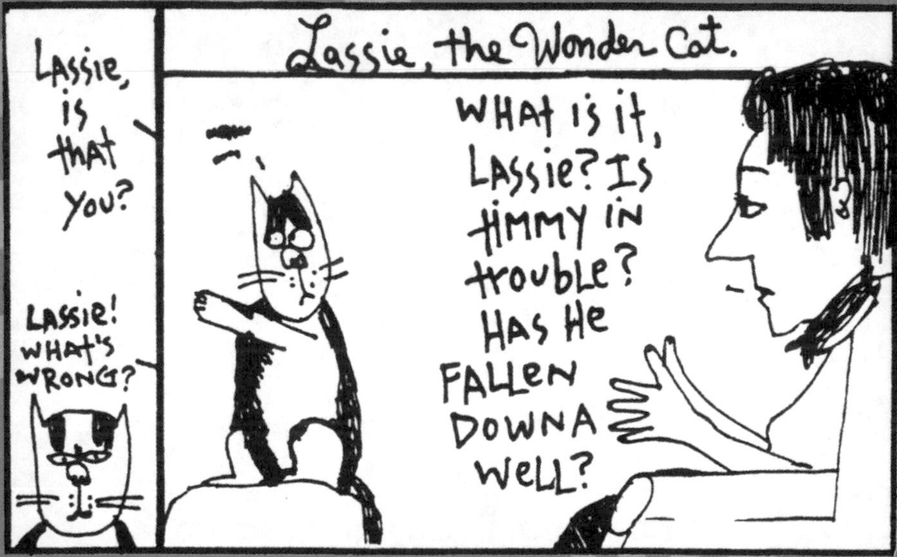
Lassie, the Wonder Cat.
LASSIE, IS THAT YOU?
LASSIE! WHAT'S WRONG?
WHAT IS IT, LASSIE? IS TIMMY IN TROUBLE? HAS HE FALLEN DOWN A WELL?

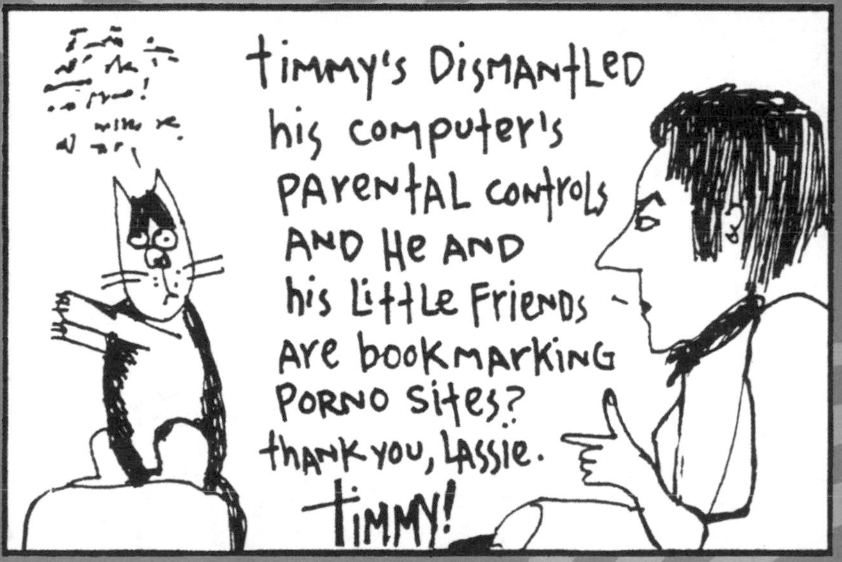
timmy's Dismantled his computer's parental controls and he and his little friends are bookmarking porno sites? thank you, Lassie.
timmy!

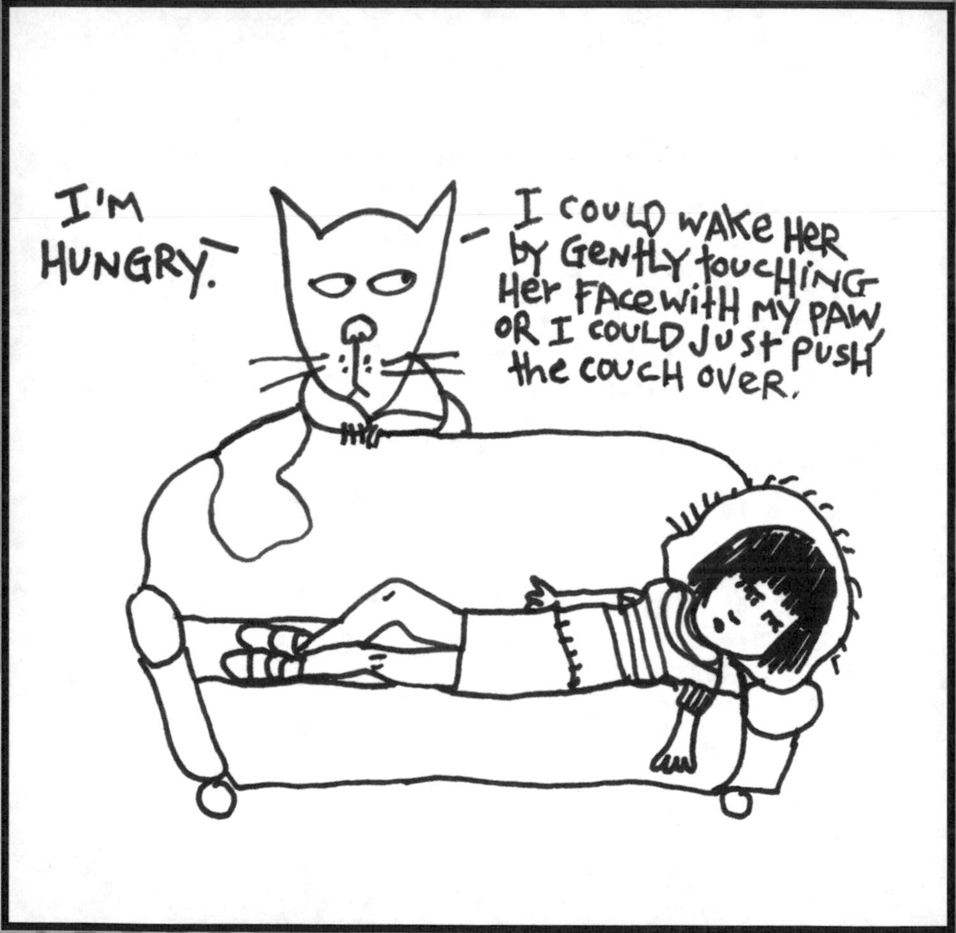
I'M HUNGRY.
I COULD WAKE HER by GENTLY touCHING Her FACE WITH MY PAW OR I COULD JUST PUSH the COUCH OVER.

SALLY, the CAT WITH ABANDONMENT ISSUES

SALLY is tAKING A NAP ON the COUCH...

BUDDY WANDERS by.

SALLY HAS A CHOICE. SHE CAN VIEW this AS AN opportuNity to GeT to KNOW BUDDY OR to GO BALListic...

Hiss Hiss Hiss Hiss Hiss Hiss Hiss Hiss Hiss

I try Not to tAKE it PersoN-ALLY

the COURAGEOUS CAT SAVES HiS beloved Mistress, ONCE AGAIN, FROM Her iDiot COUSINS.

the Door-bell... It's them...

As the DOORBELL RANG, SHE WHISPERED to me, "It's MORE of my iNbRed cousiNs. PLEASE GeT riD OF them, My GALLANT FeLiNe." I WASTED No time... LyiNG ACROSS the tHRESHOLD, I MANAGED to trip three OF Her GHASTLY KiN AND to ScRATCH A tiNy strAGGLER. RecOVERING Quickly, I DOVE FOR their SUITCASES, iNFLICTiNG HUGE GASHES beFORE SHE CALLED A GRACIOUS HALT to My ACTIONS, SENDING A SLY WINK MY WAY.

61

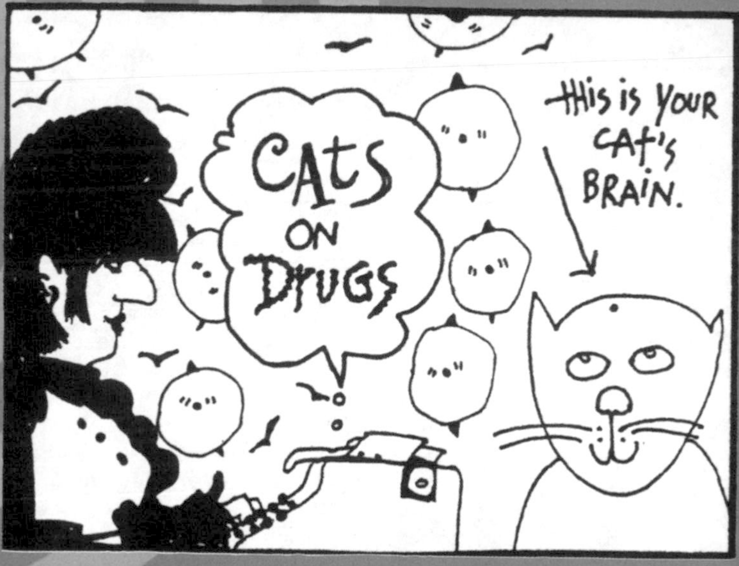
CATS ON DRUGS
THIS IS YOUR CAT'S BRAIN.

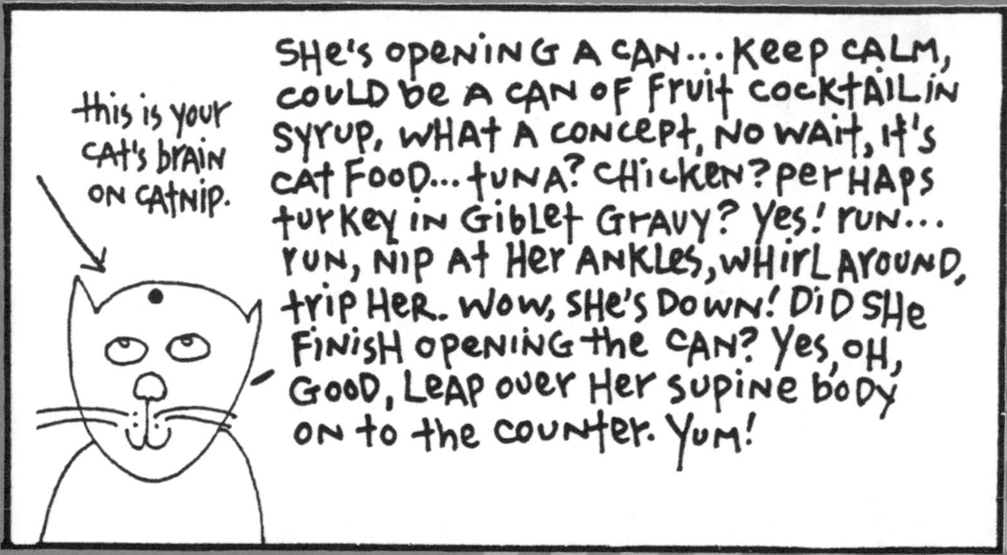
this is your cat's brain on catnip.
SHE's opening A CAN... Keep CALM, could be A CAN of fruit cocktail in syrup, WHAT A concept, No wait, it's cat Food... tuna? chicken? perhaps turkey in Giblet Gravy? yes! run... run, nip At Her ANKLES, whirl Around, trip Her. wow, SHE's Down! Did SHe Finish opening the CAN? yes, oH, Good, Leap over Her supine body on to the counter. Yum!

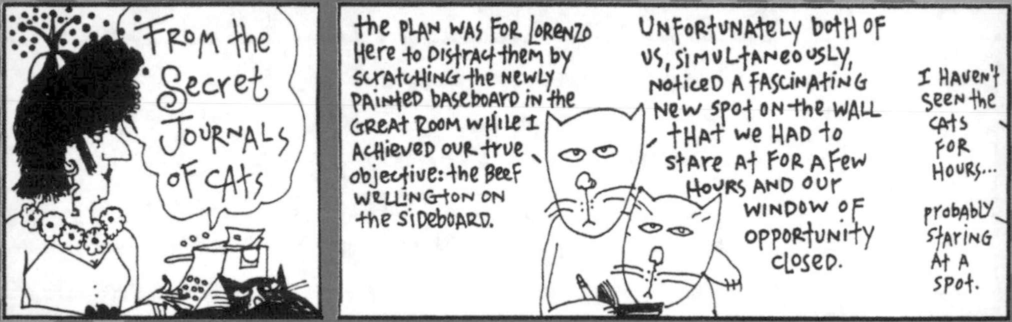
FROM the Secret JOURNALS of CATS
the PLAN WAS FOR LORENZO Here to DISTRACT them by SCRATCHING the NEWLY PAINTED baseBOARD IN the GREAT ROOM WHILE I ACHIEVED OUR true objective: the BEEF WELLINGTON ON the SIDEBOARD.
UNFORTUNATELY both OF US, SIMULTANEOUSLY, NOTICED A FASCINATING NEW SPOT ON the WALL THAT we HAD to STARE AT FOR A FEW HOURS AND OUR WINDOW OF OPPORTUNITY CLOSED.
I HAVEN'T SEEN the CATS FOR HOURS...
probably STARING AT A SPOT.

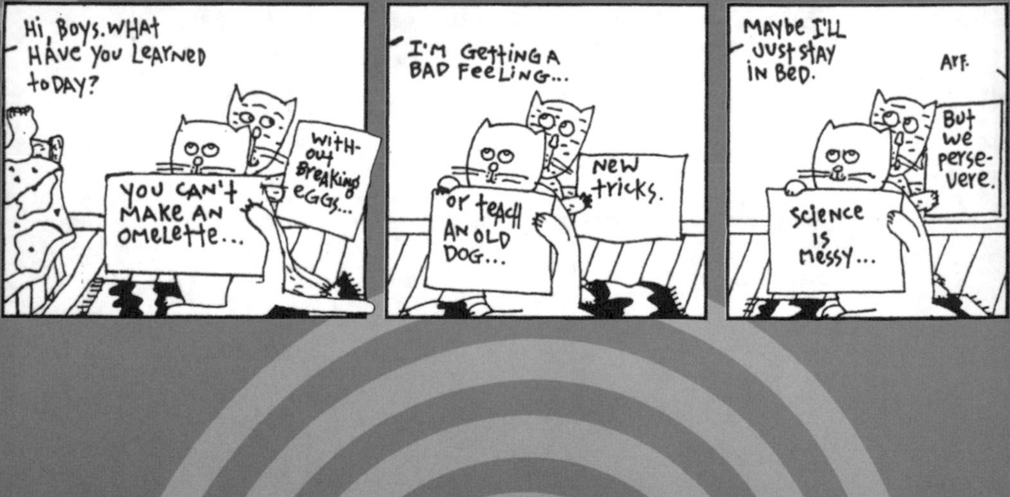
Hi, Boys. WHAT HAVE YOU LEARNED toDAY?
YOU CAN'T MAKE AN OMELETTE...
WITH-OUT BREAKING EGGS...
I'M GETTING A BAD FEELING...
OR TEACH AN OLD DOG...
NEW tricks.
MAYBE I'LL JUST STAY IN BED.
ARF.
Science is messy...
But we perse-vere.

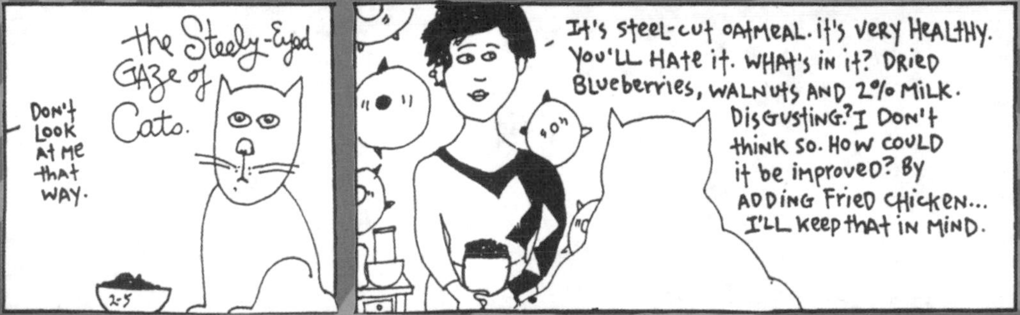
the Steely-Eyed GAZe of Cats.
Don't look at me that way.
It's steel-cut oatmeal. it's very healthy. You'll hate it. What's in it? Dried blueberries, walnuts and 2% milk. Disgusting? I don't think so. How could it be improved? By adding fried chicken... I'll keep that in mind.

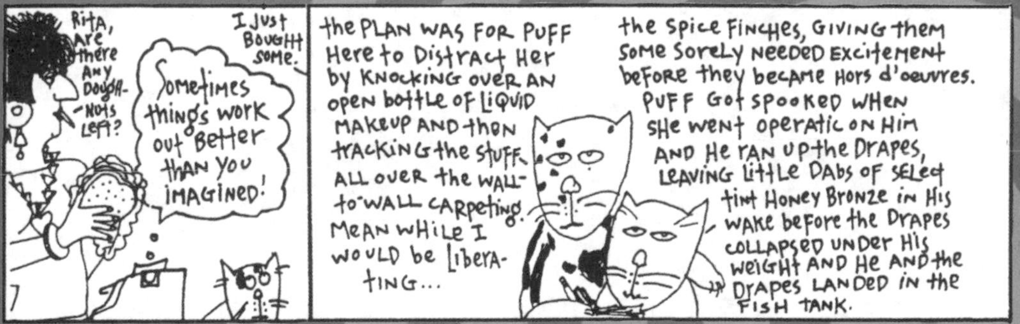
Rita, are there any dough-nuts left?
I just bought some.
Sometimes things work out better than you imagined!
the plan was for Puff here to distract her by knocking over an open bottle of liquid makeup and then tracking the stuff all over the wall-to-wall carpeting. Meanwhile I would be libera-ting...
the spice finches, giving them some sorely needed excitement before they became hors d'oeuvres.
Puff got spooked when she went operatic on him and he ran up the drapes, leaving little dabs of select tint Honey Bronze in his wake before the drapes collapsed under his weight and he and the drapes landed in the fish tank.

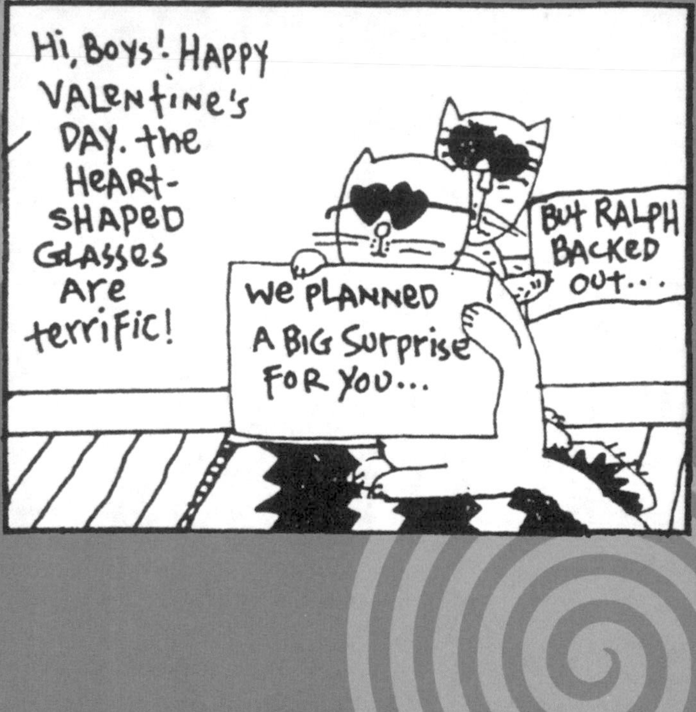
Hi, Boys! HAPPY VALENtine's DAY. the Heart-SHAPED GLASSES Are terrific!
We PLANNED A BIG Surprise FOR YOU...
But RALPH BACKED OUT...

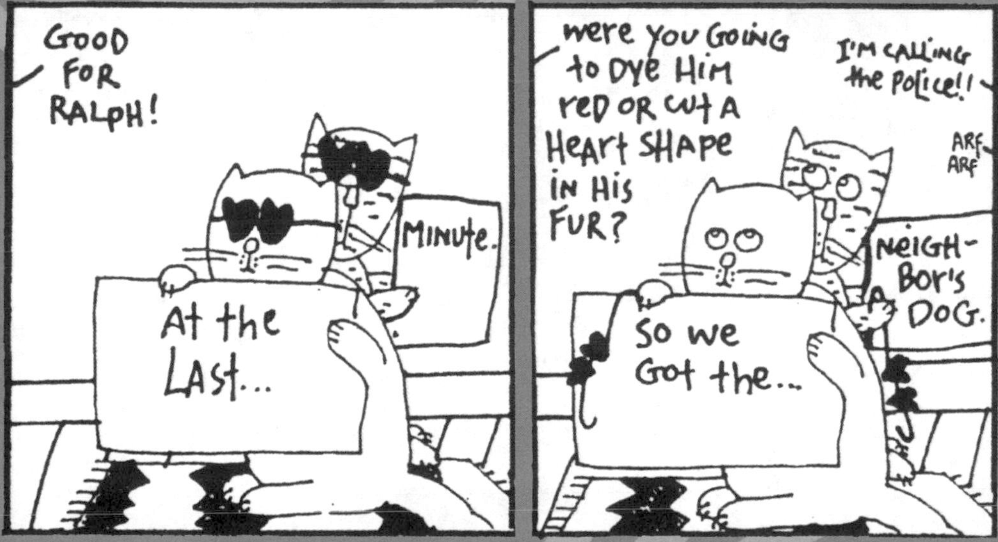
GOOD FOR RALPH!
MINUTE.
At the LAST...
were YOU GOING to DYE HIM red OR cut A Heart SHAPE IN HIS FUR?
I'M CALLING the POLICE!!
ARF ARF
NEIGH-BOR'S DOG.
So we Got the...

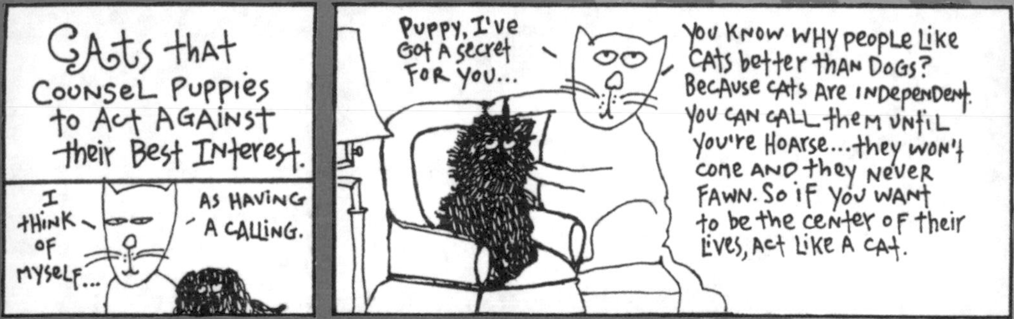
Cats that Counsel Puppies to Act Against their Best Interest.
I think of myself...
as having a calling.
Puppy, I've got a secret for you...
You know why people like cats better than dogs? Because cats are independent. You can call them until you're hoarse...they won't come and they never fawn. So if you want to be the center of their lives, act like a cat.

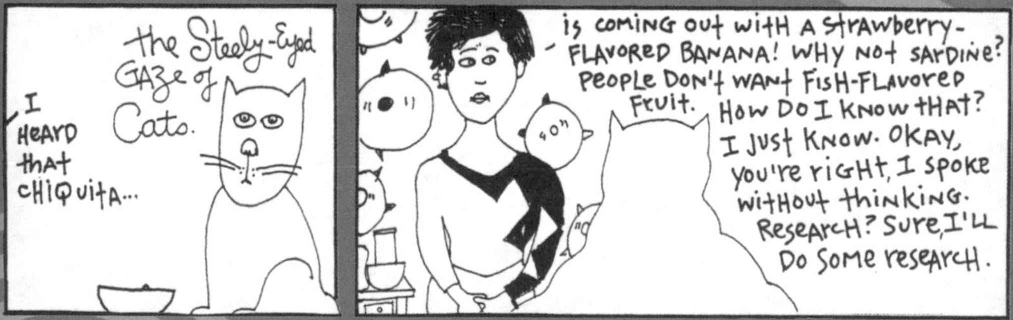
the Steely-Eyed Gaze of Cats.
I heard that Chiquita...
is coming out with a strawberry-flavored banana! Why not sardine? People don't want fish-flavored fruit. How do I know that? I just know. Okay, you're right, I spoke without thinking. Research? Sure, I'll do some research.

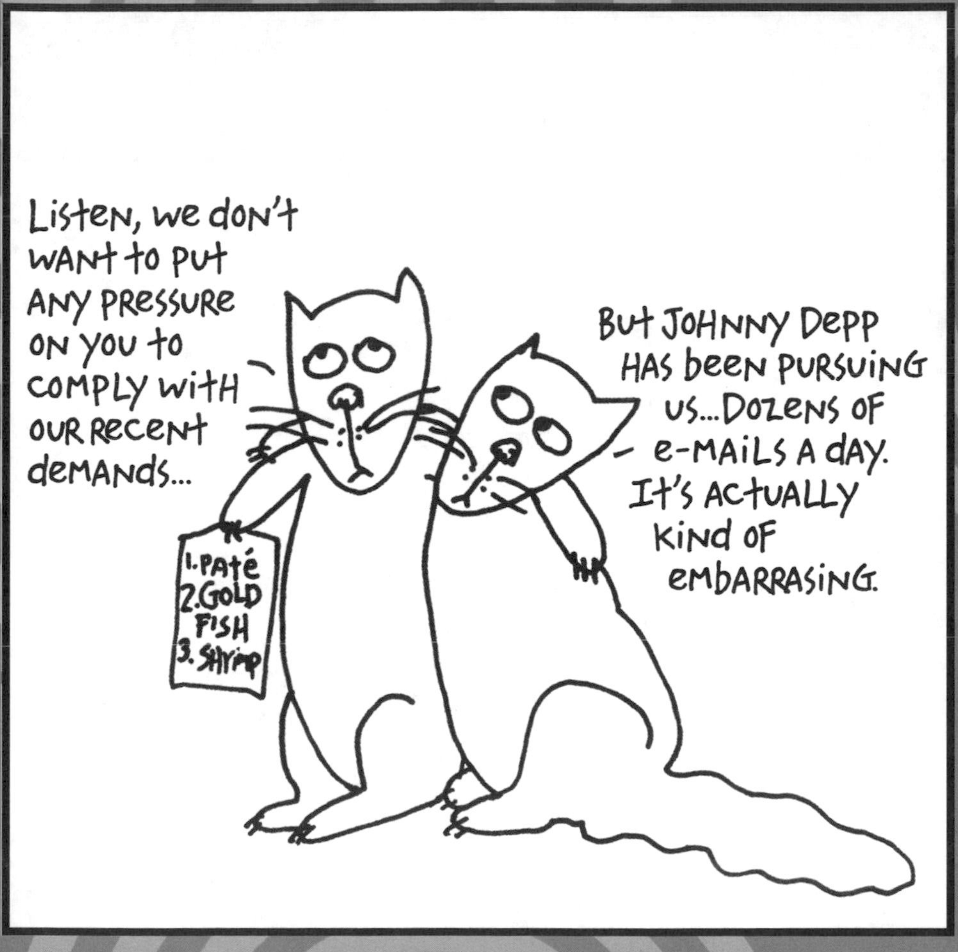
Listen, we don't want to put any pressure on you to comply with our recent demands...
1. PATÉ
2. GOLD FISH
3. SHRIMP
But JOHNNY DEPP HAS been PURSUING US...DOZENS OF e-MAILS A DAY. It's ACTUALLY kind OF embARRASING.

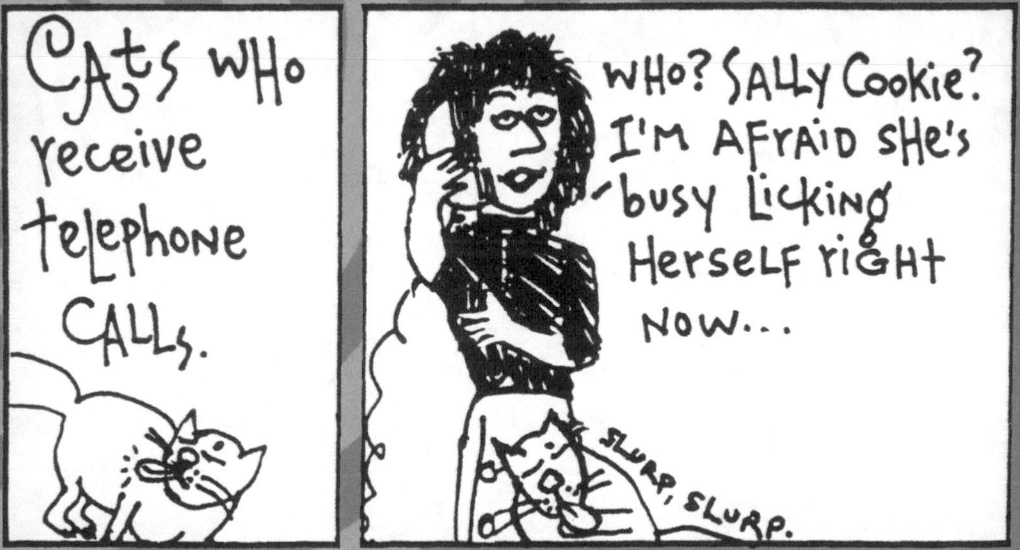
CAts WHO receive telephone CALLs.
WHO? SALLy Cookie? I'M AFRAID SHe's busy Licking Herself riGHt NOW...
SLURP, SLURP.

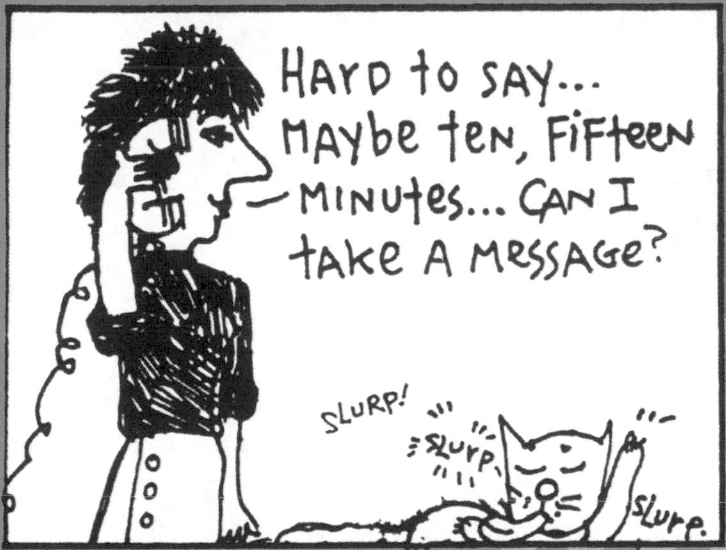
Hard to say... Maybe ten, Fifteen minutes... Can I take a message?
SLURP!
SLURP
SLURP.

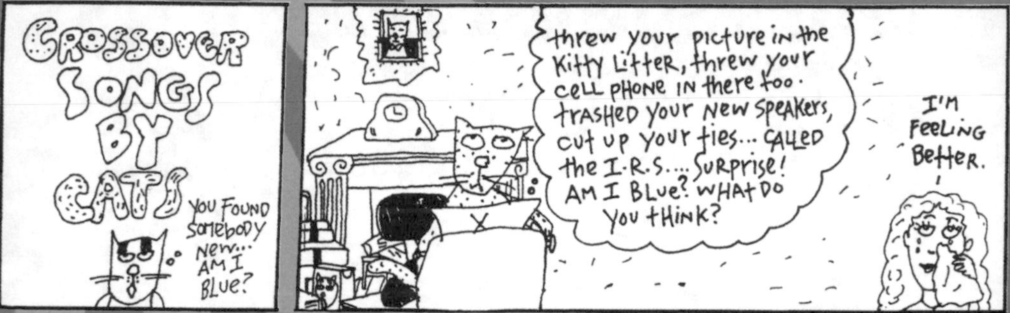
CROSSOVER SONGS BY CATS
YOU FOUND somebody new... AM I BLUE?
threw your picture in the Kitty Litter, threw your cell phone in there too. trashed your new speakers, cut up your ties... CALLED the I.R.S.... Surprise! AM I BLUE? WHAT DO YOU THINK?
I'M FEELING Better.

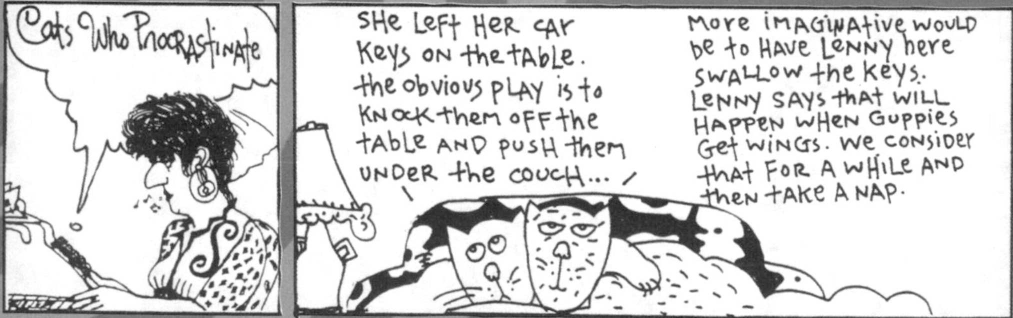
Cats Who Procrastinate
SHe Left HER car Keys on the table. the obvious play is to knock them off the table and push them under the couch...
More imaginative would be to have Lenny here swallow the keys. Lenny says that will happen when guppies get wings. We consider that for a while and then take a nap.

SALLY Cookie, the Cat with ABANDONMENT issues.

OH, NO, SHE'S GOT HER PURSE.

SALLY, I'M JUST GOING OUT FOR COFFEE...

I'LL BE BACK IN 15 MINUTES, AT THE MOST. YES, I'LL LOOK BOTH WAYS. NO, I WON'T STOP AT THE GROCERY STORE...

OKAY, I'LL MAKE COFFEE HERE.

the Kitty Olympics Volume III Victories, reCALLED.

USING the COUCH AS A TRAMPOLINE, we bounced HIGH in the Air AND LANDED ON the CHANDELIER, WHICH PUT US in PERFECT POSITION...

to LAND ON the BIRD CAGE AND KNOCK it to the GROUND, SPRINGING OPEN the DOOR AND reLEASING the birds into our WELCOMING ARMS... UNFORTUNATELY we woke the FAMILY preventing our triumphant CONSUMMATION.

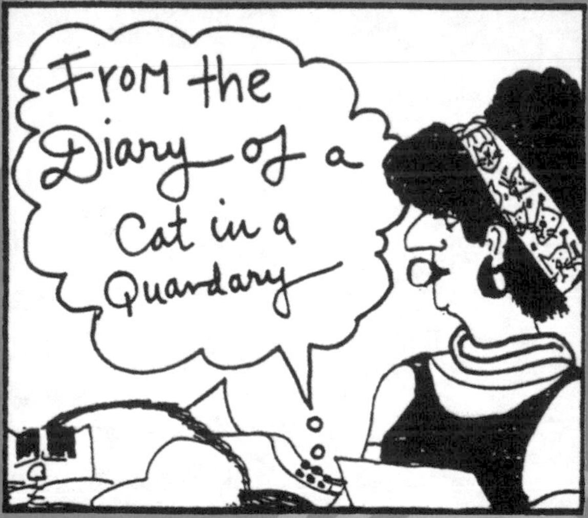
From the Diary of a Cat in a Quandary

SHE WAS ALL PACKED AND READY to LEAVE ON VACATION WHEN SHE REALIZED SHE WAS OUT OF tOOTH-PASTE... SHE'S At the StORE NOW. HERE'S MY DiLEMMA. SHOULD I UP-CHUCK iN HER SUITCASE, GiViNG HER SOMETHING to think About ON THE trip, OR GREET HER WiTH SOME HORRiBLE MESS ON HER RETURN? It'S A HARD ONE, RIGHt?

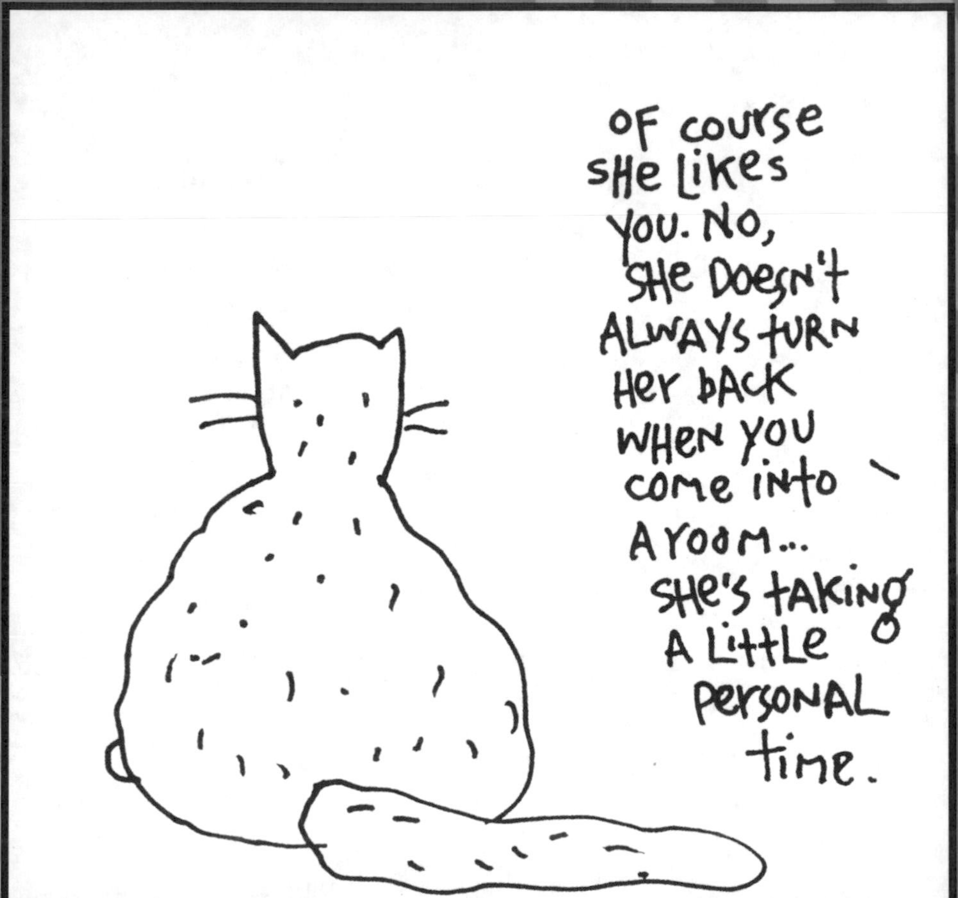
OF course SHe Likes you. No, SHe Doesn't ALWAYS turn Her back when you come into A room... SHe's taking A Little personAL time.

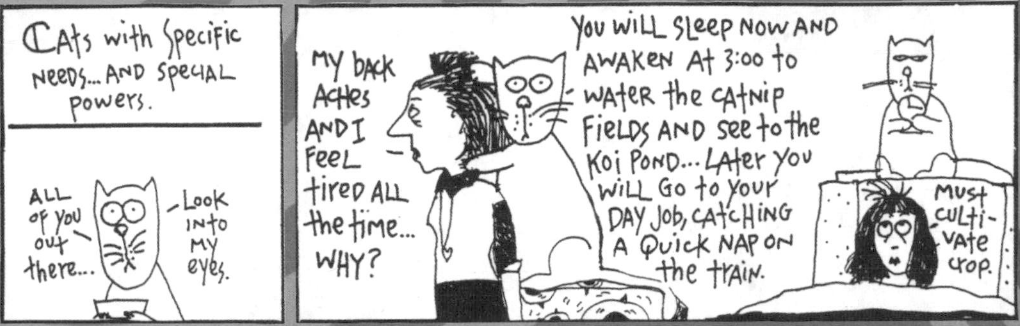
CATS with Specific NEEDS... AND SPECIAL powers.
ALL of you out there...
Look into my eyes.
MY back Aches AND I Feel tired ALL the time... WHY?
You WILL SLEEP NOW AND AWAKEN At 3:00 to water the catnip Fields AND see to the Koi POND... LAter you WILL Go to your DAY Job, CATCHING A Quick NAP ON the train.
MUST culti-vate crop.

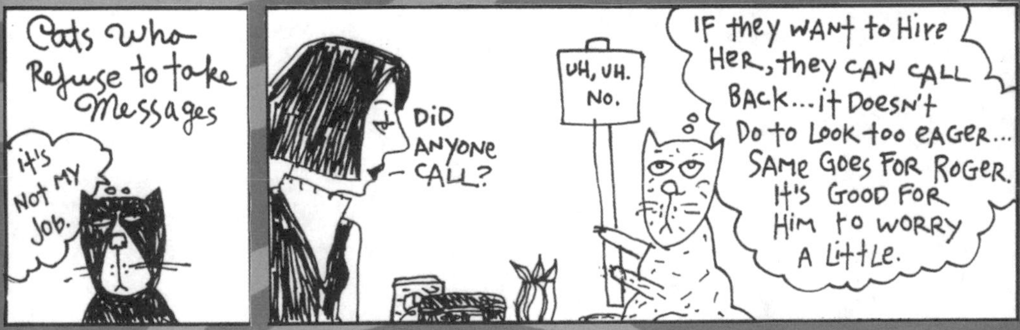
Cats who Refuse to take Messages
it's Not MY Job.
DID ANYONE CALL?
UH, UH. No.
IF they WANT to Hire Her, they CAN CALL BACK... it Doesn't Do to Look too eAGER... SAMe Goes FOR ROGER. It's GOOD FOR Him to WORRY A Little.

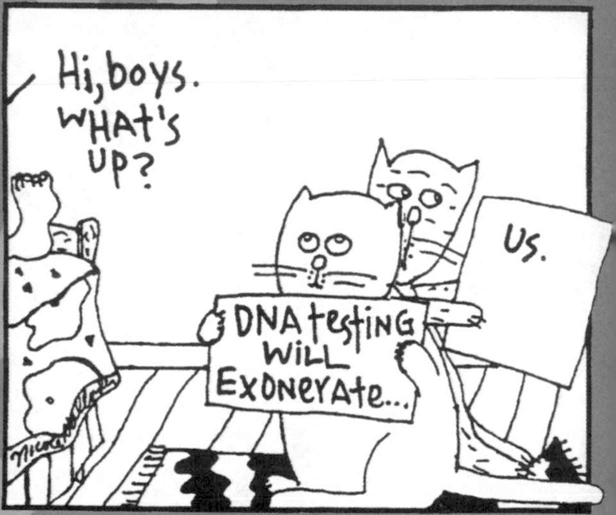
Hi, boys. WHAT'S UP?
US.
DNA testing WILL EXONERATE...

From WHAT, SpeciFiCALLY?
OH...
Boys?
ArF!
CONSULT OUR Notes.
EXCUSE US, we HAVE to...

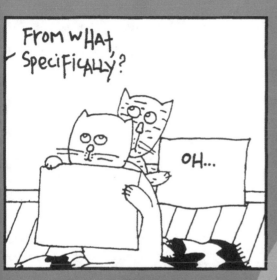

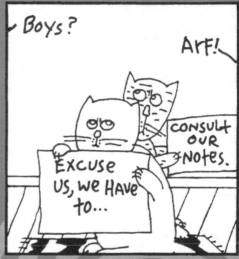

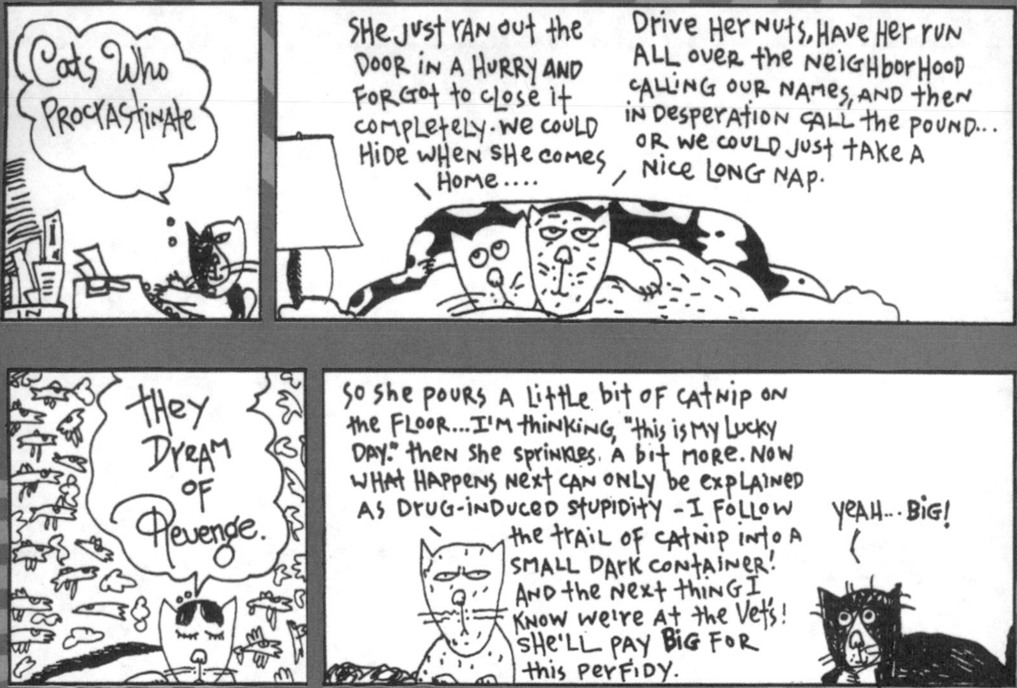
Cats Who Procrastinate
She just ran out the door in a hurry and forgot to close it completely. We could hide when she comes home....
Drive her nuts, have her run all over the neighborhood calling our names, and then in desperation call the pound... or we could just take a nice long nap.
They Dream of Revenge.
So she pours a little bit of catnip on the floor... I'm thinking, "this is my lucky day." then she sprinkles a bit more. Now what happens next can only be explained as drug-induced stupidity - I follow the trail of catnip into a small dark container! And the next thing I know we're at the Vet's! She'll pay BIG for this perfidy.
Yeah... BIG!

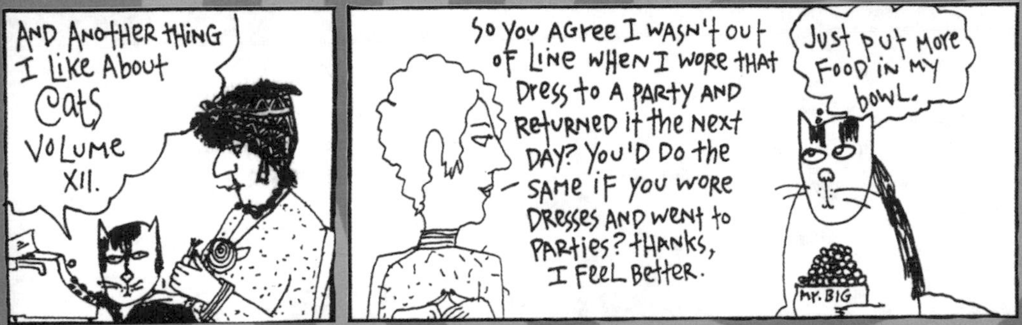
And another thing I like about Cats Volume XII.
So you agree I wasn't out of line when I wore that dress to a party and returned it the next day? You'd do the same if you wore dresses and went to parties? Thanks, I feel better.
Just put more food in my bowl.
MR. BIG

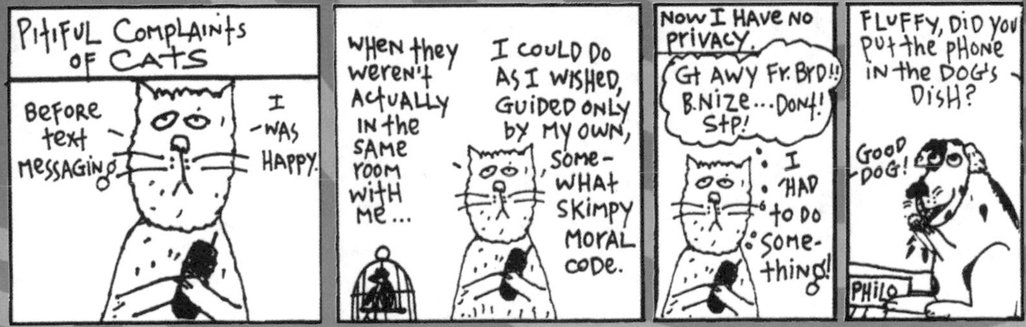
Pitiful Complaints of Cats
Before text messaging
I was happy.
When they weren't actually in the same room with me...
I could do as I wished, guided only by my own, somewhat skimpy moral code.
Now I have no privacy.
Gt awy fr. brd!! B.nize... Dont! Stp!
I had to do something!
Fluffy, did you put the phone in the dog's dish?
Good dog!
PHILO

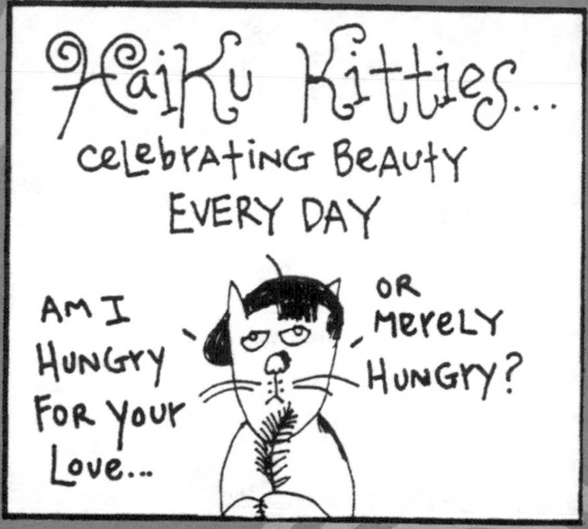
Haiku Kitties...
celebrating beauty
EVERY DAY
AM I
Hungry
For your
Love...
OR
merely
Hungry?

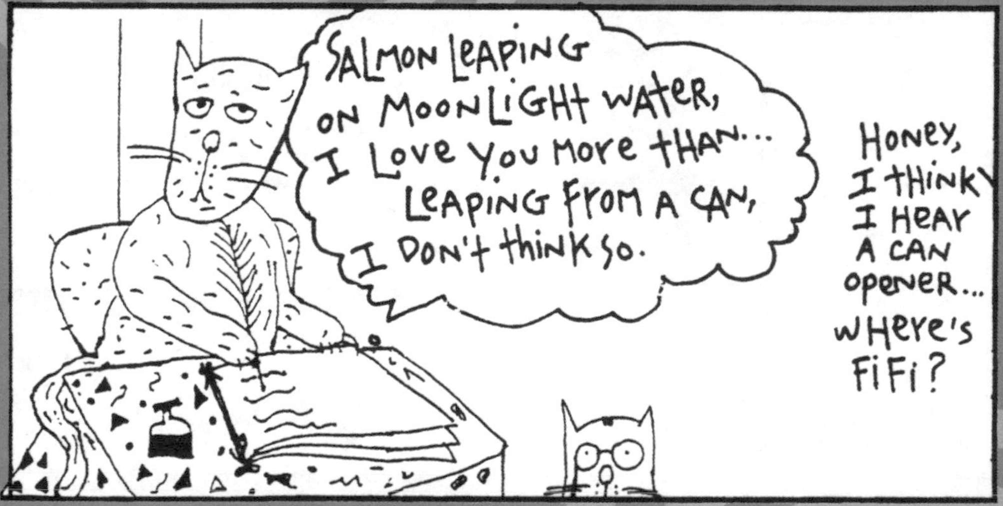
SALMON LEAPING
ON MOONLIGHT WATER,
I LOVE YOU MORE THAN...
LEAPING FROM A CAN,
I DON'T THINK SO.
Honey,
I THINK
I HEAR
A CAN
OPENER...
WHERE'S
FIFI?

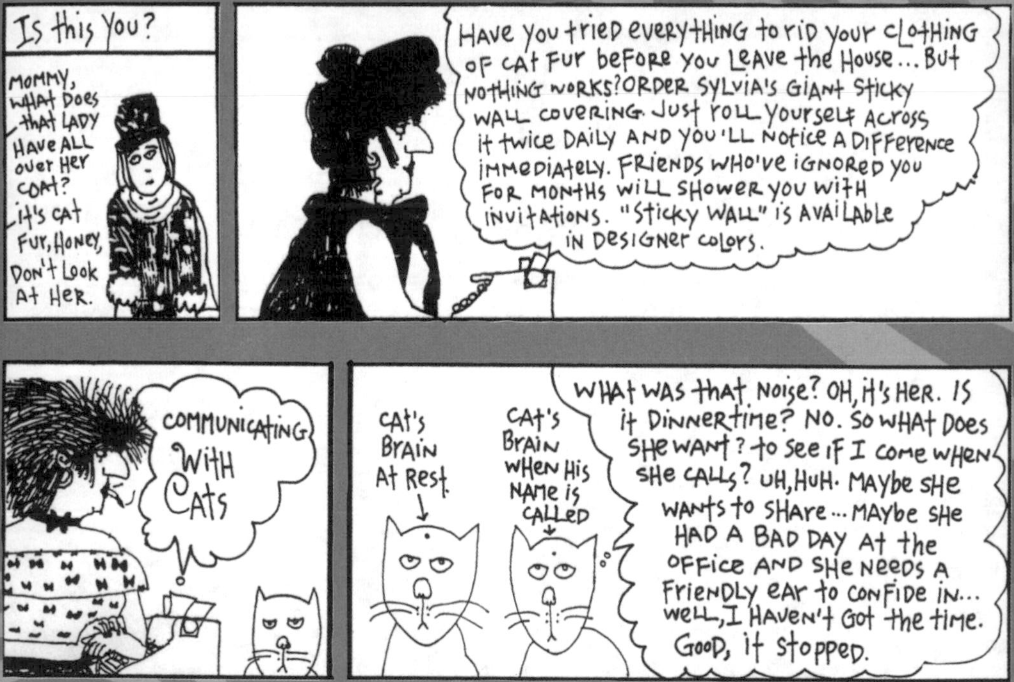
Is this You?
MOMMY, WHAT DOES THAT LADY HAVE ALL OVER HER COAT?
IT'S CAT FUR, HONEY, DON'T LOOK AT HER.
HAVE YOU TRIED EVERYTHING TO RID YOUR CLOTHING OF CAT FUR BEFORE YOU LEAVE THE HOUSE... BUT NOTHING WORKS? ORDER SYLVIA'S GIANT STICKY WALL COVERING. JUST ROLL YOURSELF ACROSS IT TWICE DAILY AND YOU'LL NOTICE A DIFFERENCE IMMEDIATELY. FRIENDS WHO'VE IGNORED YOU FOR MONTHS WILL SHOWER YOU WITH INVITATIONS. "STICKY WALL" IS AVAILABLE IN DESIGNER COLORS.
COMMUNICATING WITH CATS
CAT'S BRAIN AT REST.
CAT'S BRAIN WHEN HIS NAME IS CALLED
WHAT WAS THAT NOISE? OH, IT'S HER. IS IT DINNERTIME? NO. SO WHAT DOES SHE WANT? TO SEE IF I COME WHEN SHE CALLS? UH, HUH. MAYBE SHE WANTS TO SHARE... MAYBE SHE HAD A BAD DAY AT THE OFFICE AND SHE NEEDS A FRIENDLY EAR TO CONFIDE IN... WELL, I HAVEN'T GOT THE TIME. GOOD, IT STOPPED.

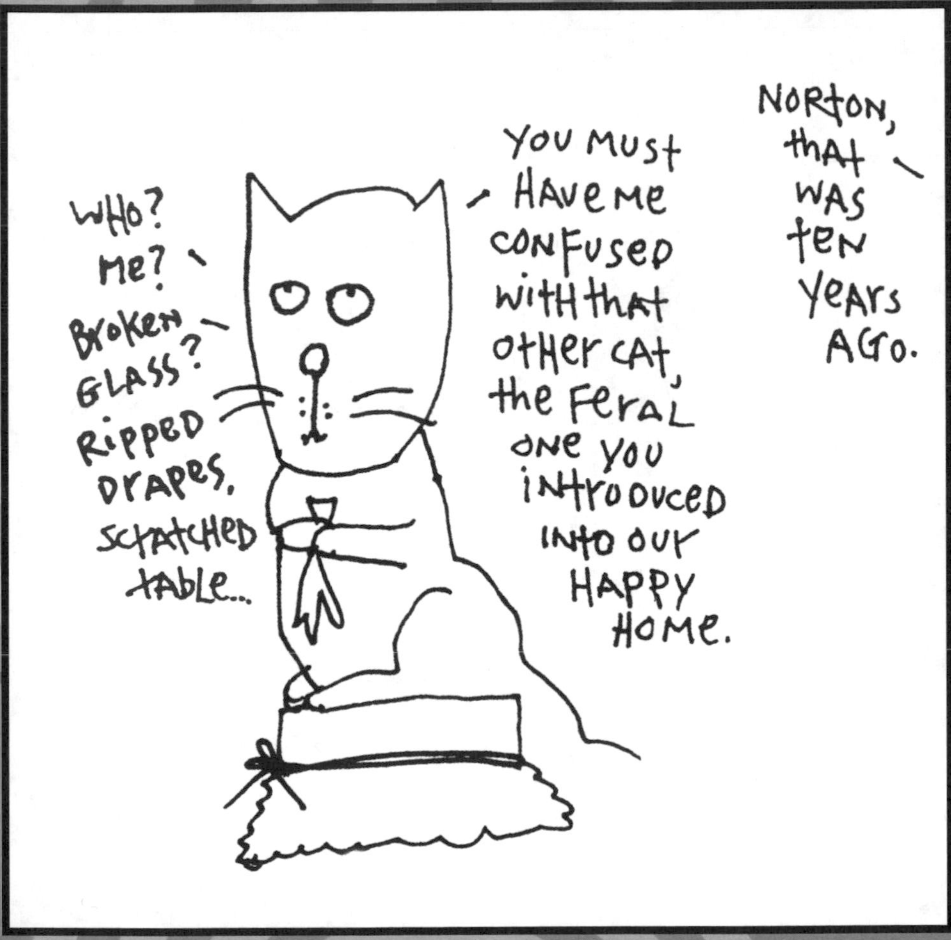
WHO? ME? BROKEN GLASS? RIPPED DRAPES, SCRATCHED TABLE...
YOU MUST HAVE ME CONFUSED WITH THAT OTHER CAT, THE FERAL ONE YOU INTRODUCED INTO OUR HAPPY HOME.
NORTON, THAT WAS TEN YEARS AGO.

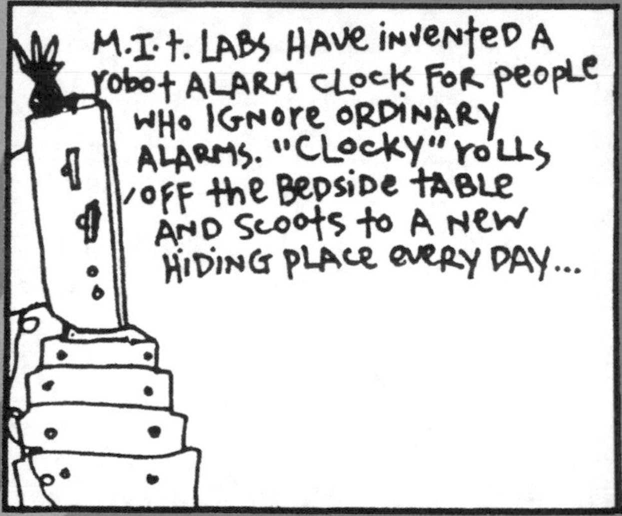
M.I.T. LABS HAVE INVENTED A ROBOT ALARM CLOCK FOR PEOPLE WHO IGNORE ORDINARY ALARMS. "CLOCKY" ROLLS OFF THE BEDSIDE TABLE AND SCOOTS TO A NEW HIDING PLACE EVERY DAY...

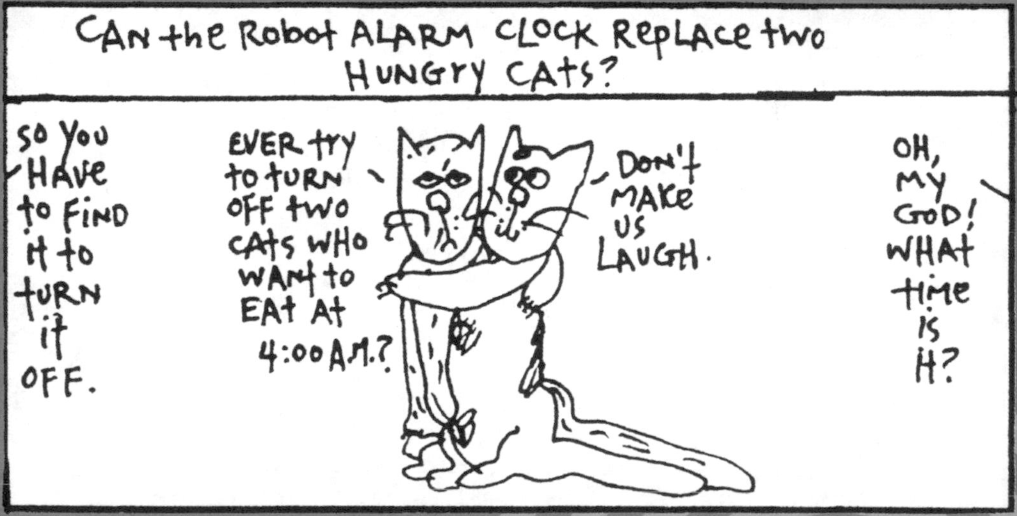
CAN the Robot ALARM CLOCK RepLACe two HUNGry CATs?
SO YOU HAVE to FIND it to turn it OFF.
EVER try to turn OFF two cats who want to eat at 4:00 A.M.?
Don't make us laugh.
OH, MY GOD! WHAT time is it?

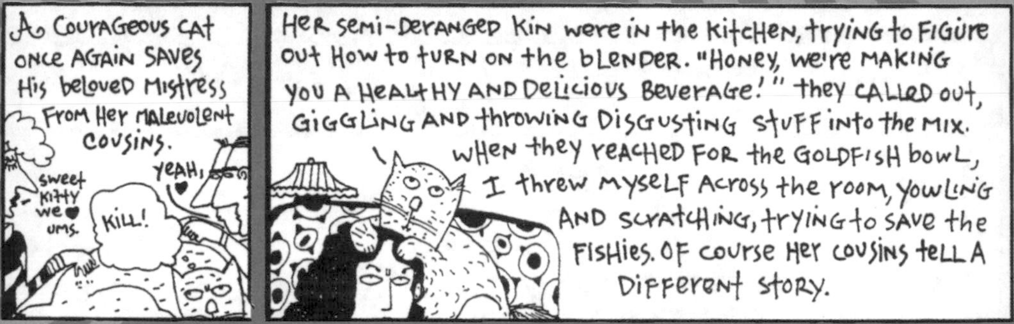
A Courageous cat once again saves his beloved Mistress from her malevolent cousins.
sweet kitty we ♥ ums.
KILL!
YEAH, ♥
Her semi-deranged kin were in the kitchen, trying to figure out how to turn on the blender. "Honey, we're making you a healthy and delicious beverage!" they called out, giggling and throwing disgusting stuff into the mix. When they reached for the goldfish bowl, I threw myself across the room, yowling and scratching, trying to save the fishies. Of course her cousins tell a different story.

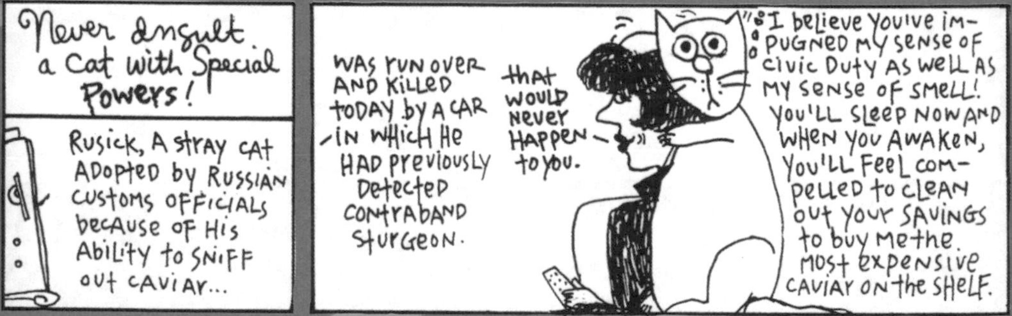
Never Insult a Cat with Special Powers!
Rusick, a stray cat adopted by Russian customs officials because of his ability to sniff out caviar...
was run over and killed today by a car in which he had previously detected contraband sturgeon.
that would never happen to you.
"I believe you've impugned my sense of civic duty as well as my sense of smell! You'll sleep now and when you awaken, you'll feel compelled to clean out your savings to buy me the most expensive caviar on the shelf.

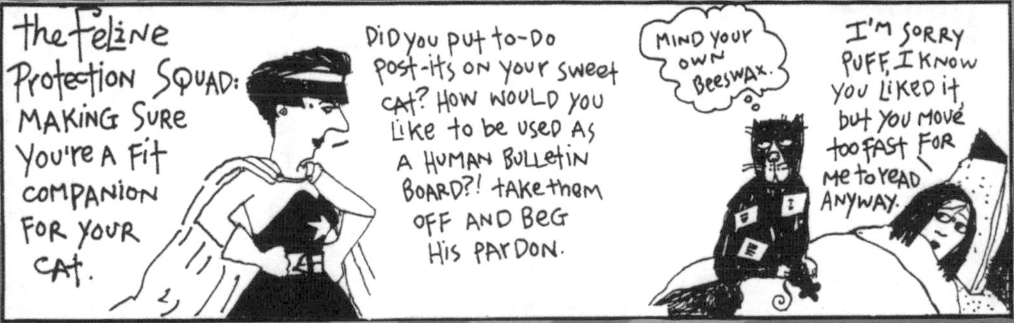
the Feline Protection Squad: MAKING Sure you're A Fit companion FOR your cat.
DID you put to-Do post-its on your sweet cat? HOW WOULD you Like to be used As A HUMAN Bulletin BOARD?! take them OFF AND Beg His PArDON.
MIND your own Beeswax.
I'm SORRY PUFF, I KNOW you LikeD it, but you move too FAST FOR me to read ANYWAY.

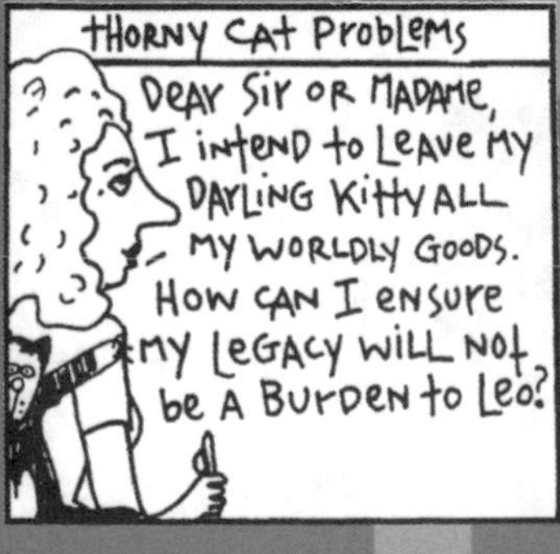
tHORNY CAt ProbLems
Dear Sir OR MADAME, I intend to Leave my DARLING Kitty ALL my WORLDLY GOODS. How can I ensure my Legacy will not be A Burden to Leo?

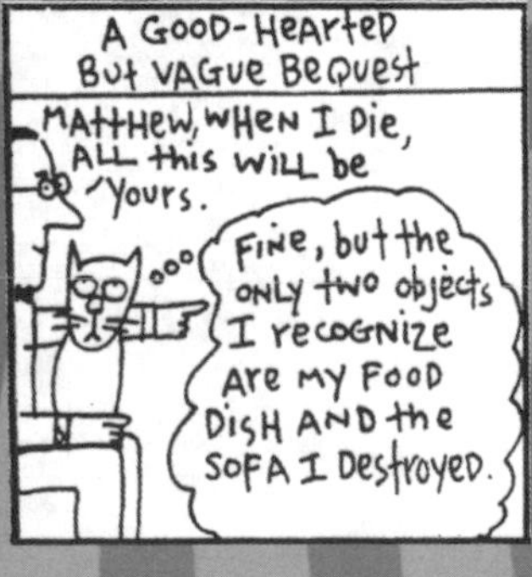
A GOOD-HeArteD But VAGUE BeQuest
MAtthew, wHEN I Die, ALL this will be yours.
Fine, but the only two objects I recognize Are my FOOD DiSH AND the SOFA I Destroyed.

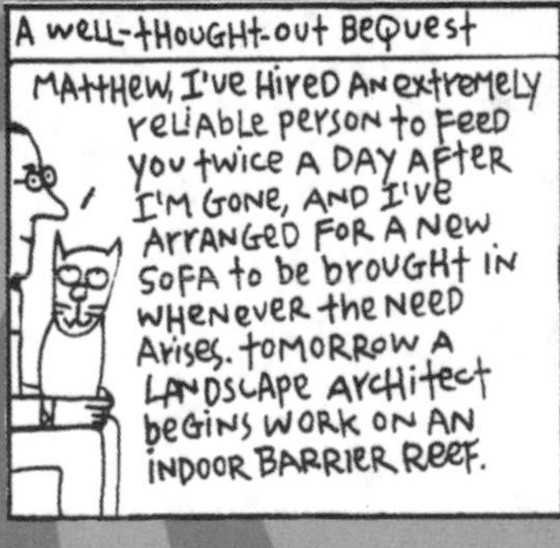
A well-thought-out BeQuest
MAtthew, I've Hired An extremely reliable person to Feed you twice A DAY After I'm Gone, AND I've ArrANGeD FOR A New SOFA to be brought in whenever the Need Arises. tomorrow A LANDSCAPE Architect begins work on an indoor BARRIER Reef.

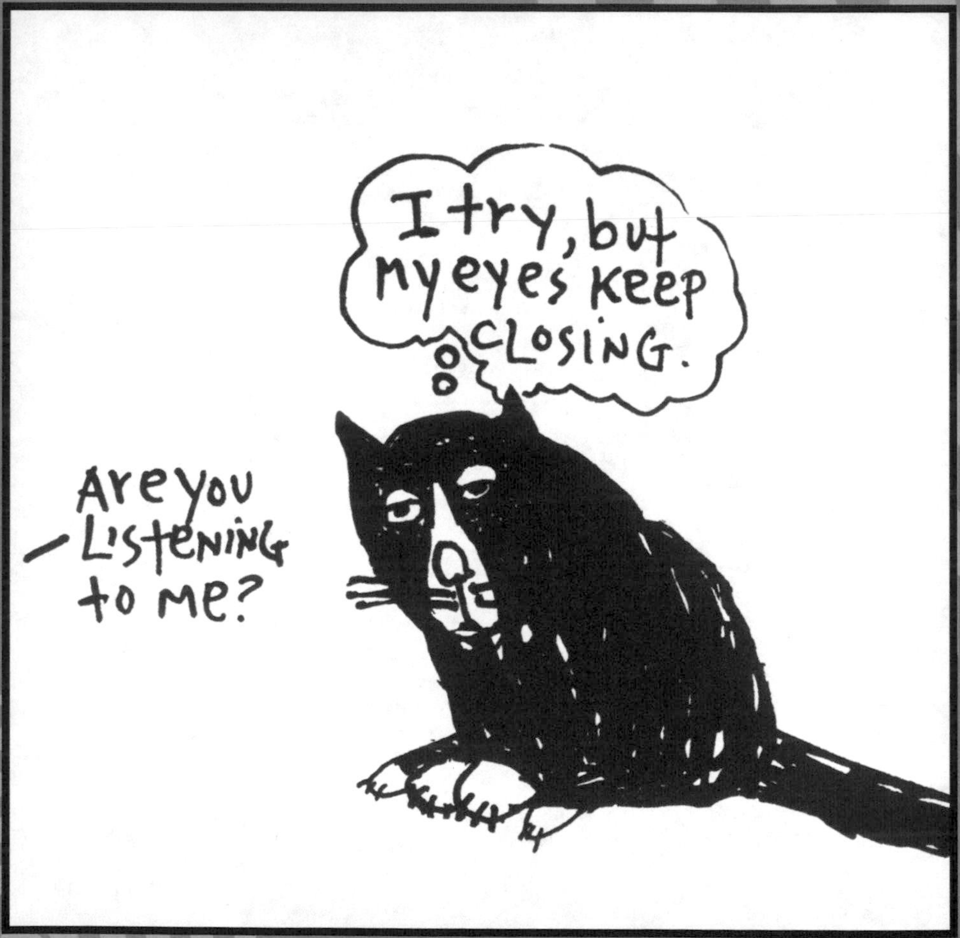
I try, but my eyes keep closing.
Are you listening to me?

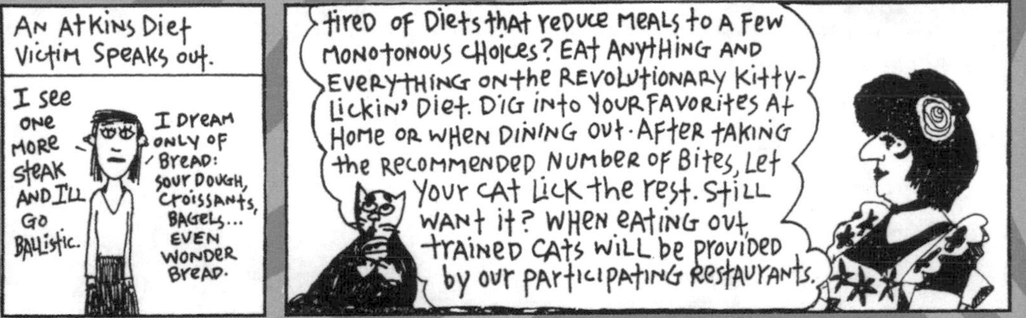
An Atkins Diet Victim Speaks out.
I see one more steak and I'll go ballistic.
I dream only of bread: sour dough, croissants, bagels... even Wonder Bread.
tired of Diets that reduce meals to a few monotonous choices? Eat anything and everything on the Revolutionary Kitty-Lickin' Diet. Dig into your favorites at home or when dining out. After taking the recommended number of bites, let your cat lick the rest. Still want it? When eating out, trained cats will be provided by our participating restaurants.

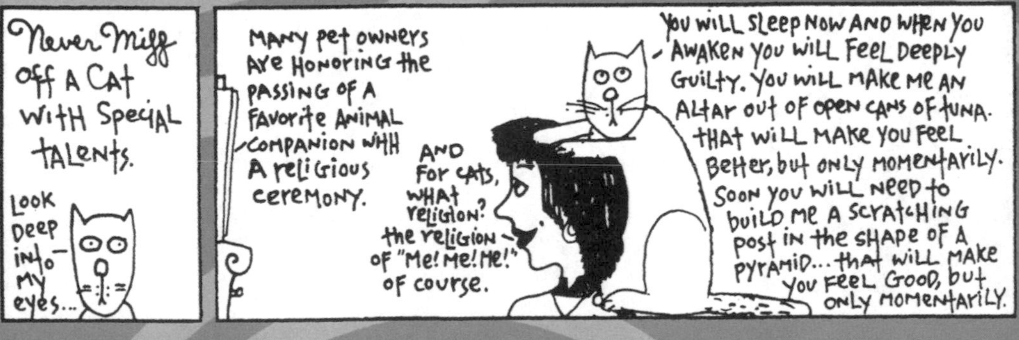
Never Miff off a Cat with Special talents.
Look deep into my eyes...
Many pet owners are honoring the passing of a favorite animal companion with a religious ceremony.
And for cats, what religion?
the religion of "Me! Me! Me!" of course.
You will sleep now and when you awaken you will feel deeply guilty. You will make me an altar out of open cans of tuna. That will make you feel better, but only momentarily. Soon you will need to build me a scratching post in the shape of a pyramid... that will make you feel good, but only momentarily.

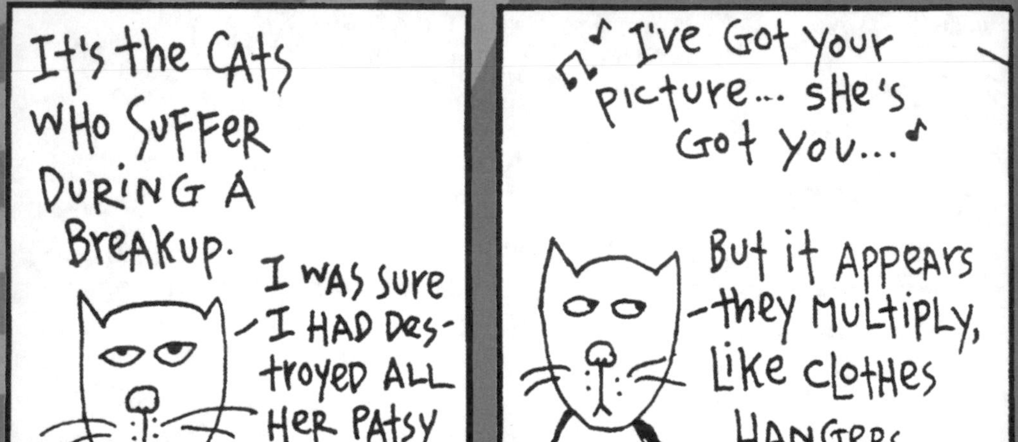
It's the Cats who Suffer during a Breakup.
I was sure I had destroyed all her Patsy Cline CDs.
♫♪ I've Got your picture... she's Got you...♪
But it appears they multiply, like clothes hangers.

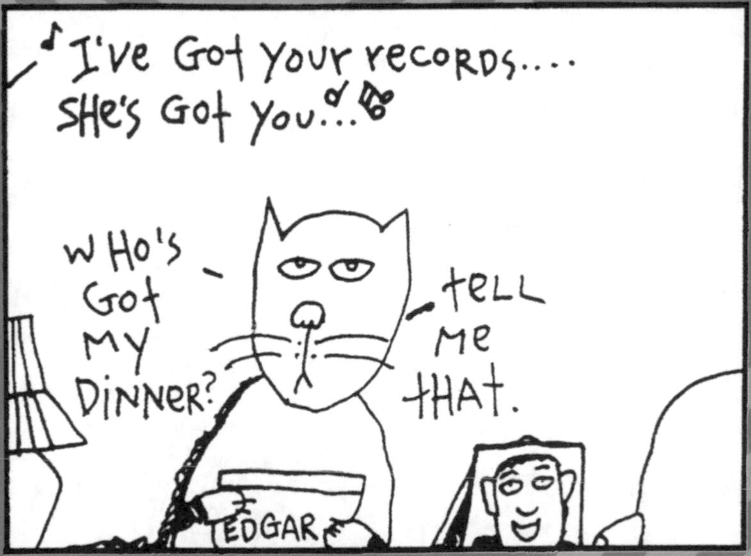
I've Got your records....
SHe's Got you...
WHo's Got My Dinner?
tell me that.
EDGAR

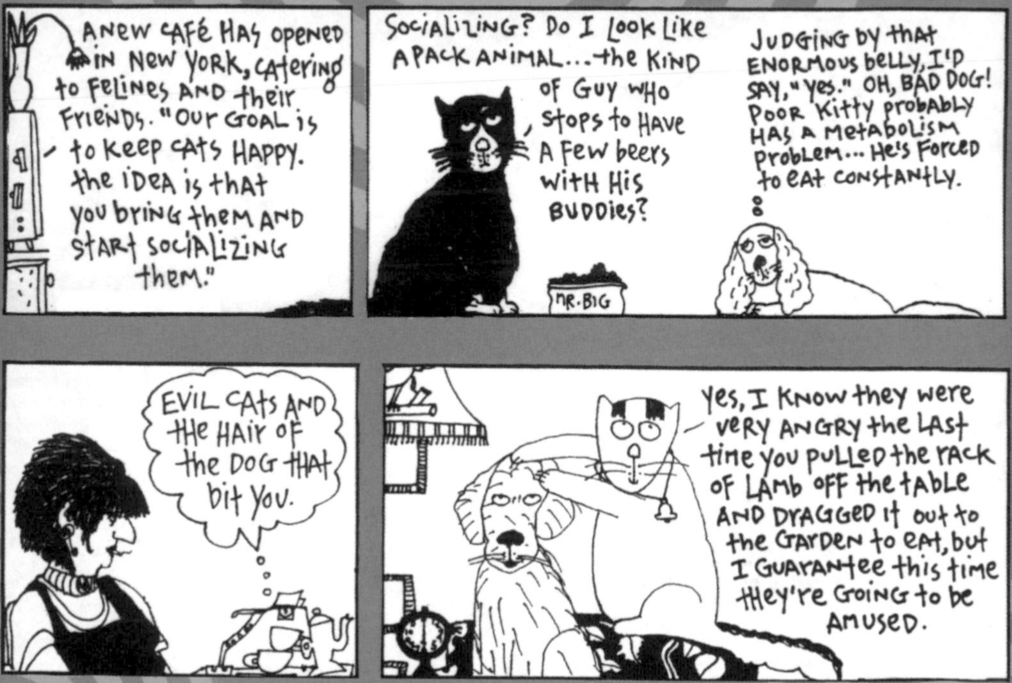
A new café has opened in New York, catering to felines and their friends. "Our goal is to keep cats happy. The idea is that you bring them and start socializing them."
Socializing? Do I look like a pack animal... the kind of guy who stops to have a few beers with his buddies?
MR. BIG
Judging by that enormous belly, I'd say, "yes." Oh, bad dog! Poor kitty probably has a metabolism problem... He's forced to eat constantly.
Evil cats and the hair of the dog that bit you.
Yes, I know they were very angry the last time you pulled the rack of lamb off the table and dragged it out to the garden to eat, but I guarantee this time they're going to be amused.

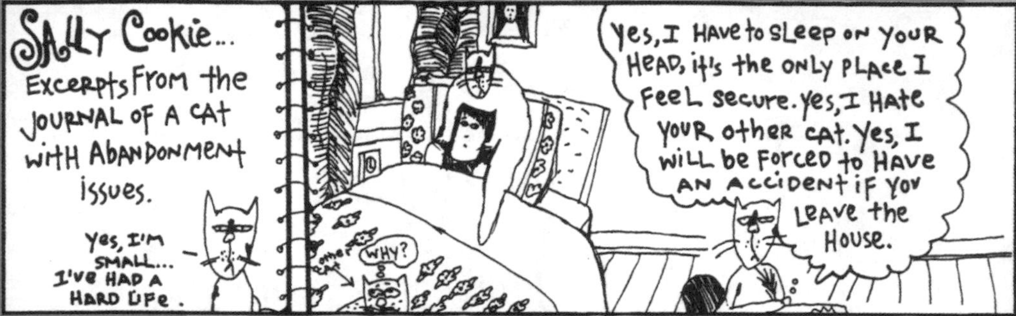
SALLY COOKIE...
EXCERPTS FROM THE JOURNAL OF A CAT WITH ABANDONMENT ISSUES.
YES, I'M SMALL... I'VE HAD A HARD LIFE.
OTHER CAT
WHY?
YES, I HAVE TO SLEEP ON YOUR HEAD, IT'S THE ONLY PLACE I FEEL SECURE. YES, I HATE YOUR OTHER CAT. YES, I WILL BE FORCED TO HAVE AN ACCIDENT IF YOU LEAVE THE HOUSE.

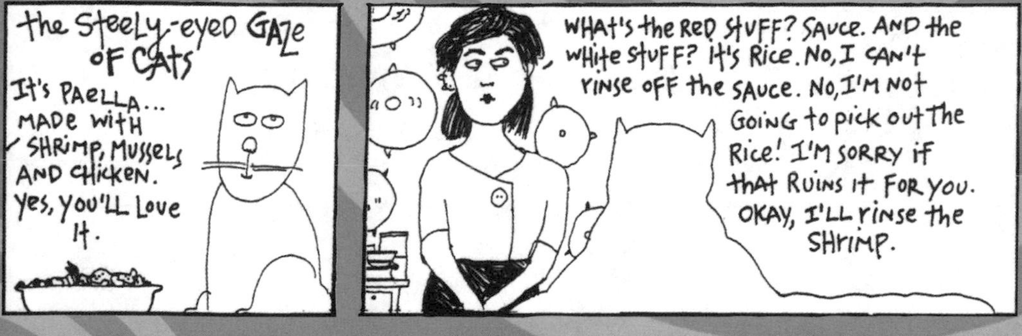
THE STEELY-EYED GAZE OF CATS
IT'S PAELLA... MADE WITH SHRIMP, MUSSELS AND CHICKEN. YES, YOU'LL LOVE IT.
WHAT'S THE RED STUFF? SAUCE. AND THE WHITE STUFF? IT'S RICE. NO, I CAN'T RINSE OFF THE SAUCE. NO, I'M NOT GOING TO PICK OUT THE RICE! I'M SORRY IF THAT RUINS IT FOR YOU. OKAY, I'LL RINSE THE SHRIMP.

A CAT'S Attitude TOWARD the FOOD OF OTHERS.

WHAT's MINE is YOURS, WHAT's YOURS is MINE. I'LL TAKE THAT FRIED CHICKEN ON YOUR PLATE, AND YOU CAN HAVE THE BROWN STUFF YOU SERVE ME.

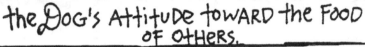

the Dog's Attitude toward the Food of Others.

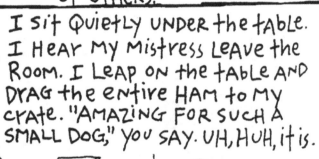

I sit Quietly under the table. I hear my mistress leave the room. I leap on the table and drag the entire ham to my crate. "Amazing for such a small dog," you say. Uh, huh, it is.

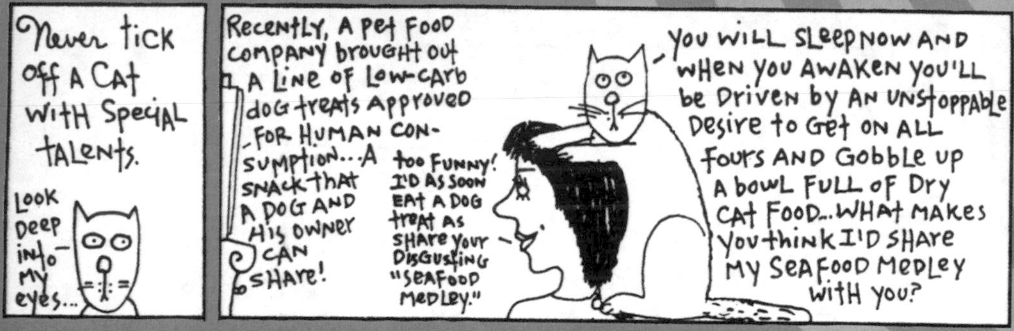
Never tick off a Cat with Special talents.
Look deep into my eyes...
Recently, a pet food company brought out a line of low-carb dog treats approved for human consumption... A snack that a dog and his owner can share!
Too funny! I'd as soon eat a dog treat as share your disgusting "Seafood Medley."
You will sleep now and when you awaken you'll be driven by an unstoppable desire to get on all fours and gobble up a bowl full of dry cat food... What makes you think I'd share my Seafood Medley with you?

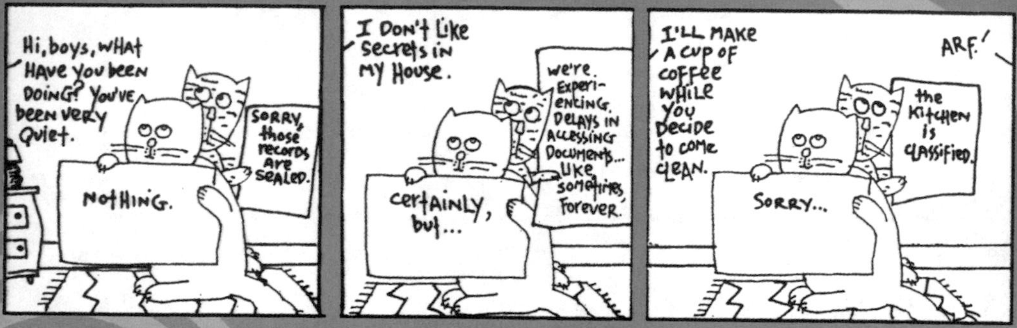
Hi, boys, what have you been doing? You've been very quiet.
Nothing.
Sorry, those records are sealed.
I don't like secrets in my house.
Certainly, but...
We're experiencing delays in accessing documents... like, sometimes, forever.
I'll make a cup of coffee while you decide to come clean.
Sorry...
The kitchen is classified.
Arf!

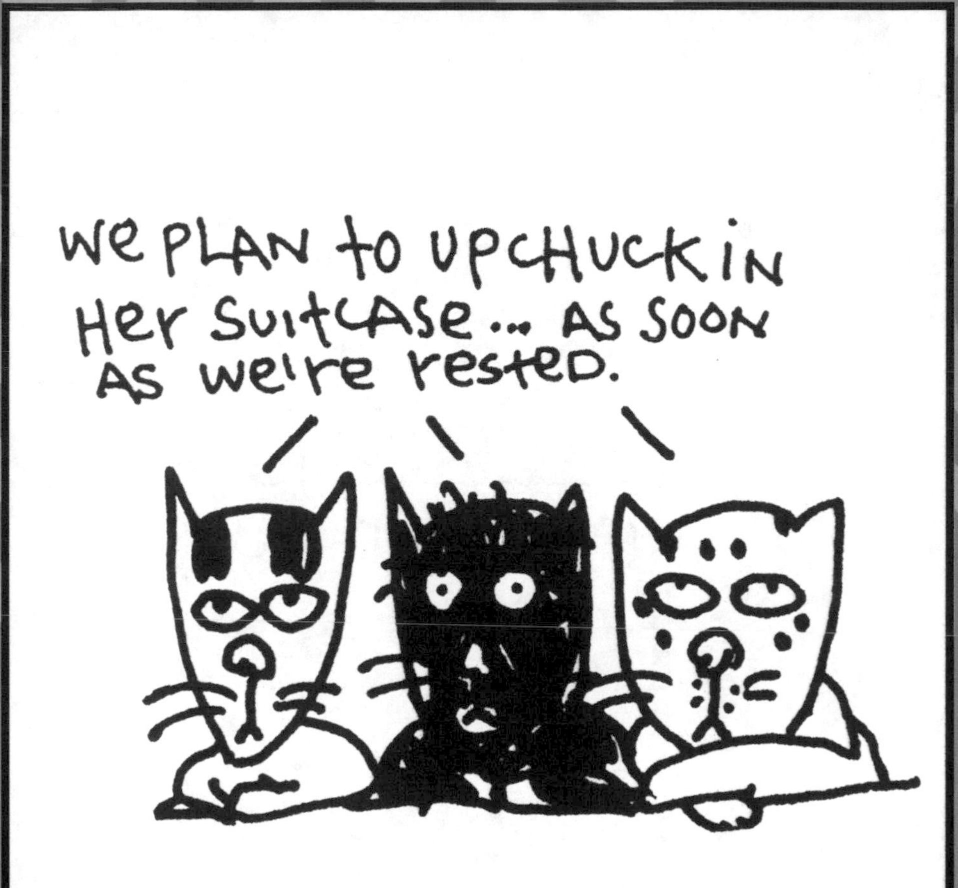
WE PLAN TO UPCHUCK IN HER SUITCASE... AS SOON AS WE'RE RESTED.

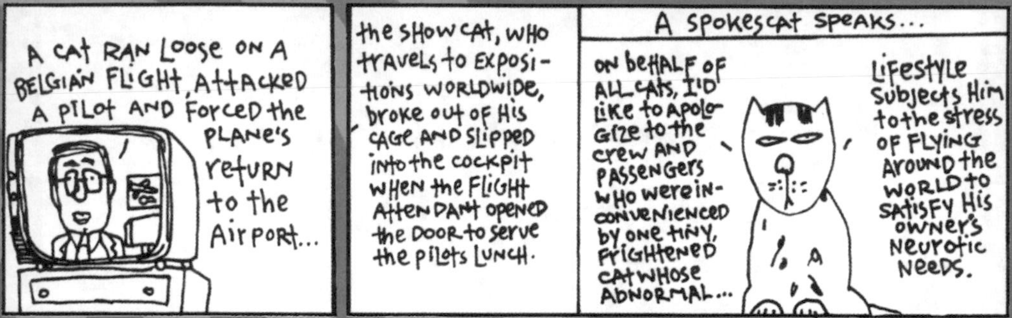
A CAT RAN LOOSE ON A BELGIAN FLIGHT, ATTACKED A PILOT AND FORCED THE PLANE'S RETURN TO THE AIRPORT...
THE SHOW CAT, WHO TRAVELS TO EXPOSITIONS WORLDWIDE, BROKE OUT OF HIS CAGE AND SLIPPED INTO THE COCKPIT WHEN THE FLIGHT ATTENDANT OPENED THE DOOR TO SERVE THE PILOTS LUNCH.
A SPOKESCAT SPEAKS...
ON BEHALF OF ALL CATS, I'D LIKE TO APOLOGIZE TO THE CREW AND PASSENGERS WHO WERE INCONVENIENCED BY ONE TINY, FRIGHTENED CAT WHOSE ABNORMAL...
LIFESTYLE SUBJECTS HIM TO THE STRESS OF FLYING AROUND THE WORLD TO SATISFY HIS OWNER'S NEUROTIC NEEDS.

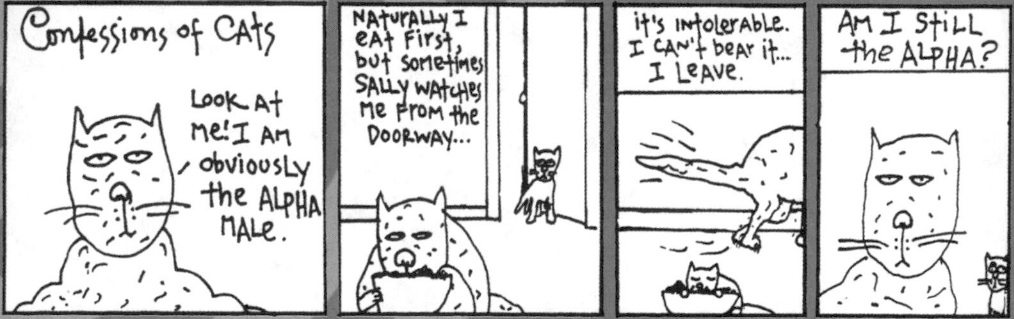
Confessions of Cats
LOOK AT ME! I AM OBVIOUSLY THE ALPHA MALE.
NATURALLY I EAT FIRST, BUT SOMETIMES SALLY WATCHES ME FROM THE DOORWAY...
IT'S INTOLERABLE. I CAN'T BEAR IT... I LEAVE.
AM I STILL THE ALPHA?

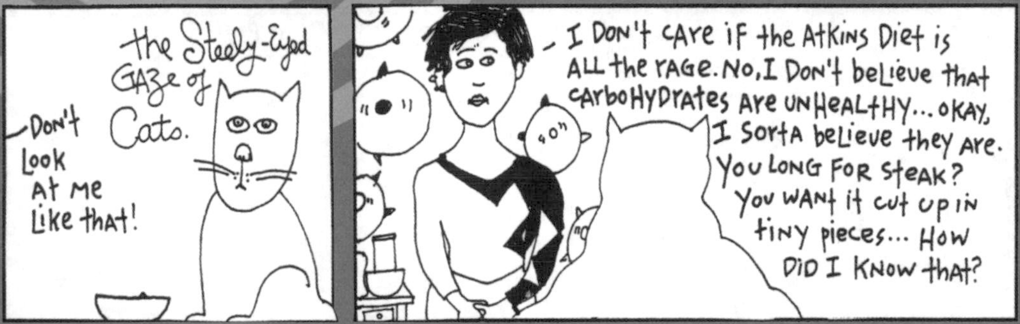
the Steely-Eyed GAZe of Cats.
Don't look At me Like that!
I DON'T CARE IF THE ATKINS DIET IS ALL THE RAGE. NO, I DON'T BELIEVE THAT CARBOHYDRATES ARE UNHEALTHY... OKAY, I SORTA BELIEVE THEY ARE. YOU LONG FOR STEAK? YOU WANT IT CUT UP IN TINY PIECES... HOW DID I KNOW THAT?

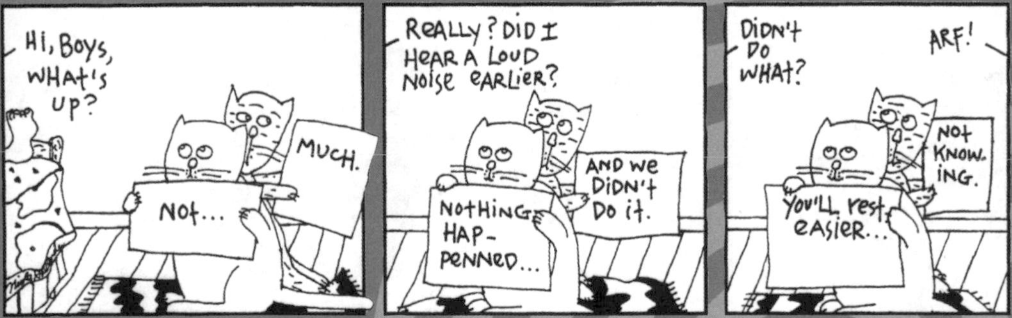
HI, BOYS, WHAT'S UP?
NOT...
MUCH.
REALLY? DID I HEAR A LOUD NOISE EARLIER?
NOTHING HAP-PENNED...
AND WE DIDN'T DO IT.
DIDN'T DO WHAT?
ARF!
YOU'LL REST EASIER...
NOT KNOW-ING.

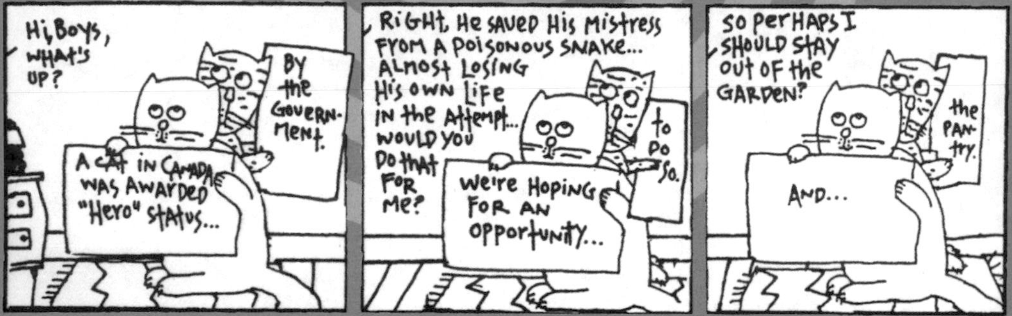

Hi, Boys, what's up?
A cat in Canada was awarded "Hero" status...
By the Govern-ment.
Right, He saved His Mistress from a poisonous snake... almost losing His own Life in the Attempt... would you do that for me?
We're hoping for an opportunity...
to do so.
So perhaps I should stay out of the garden?
And...
the pan-try.

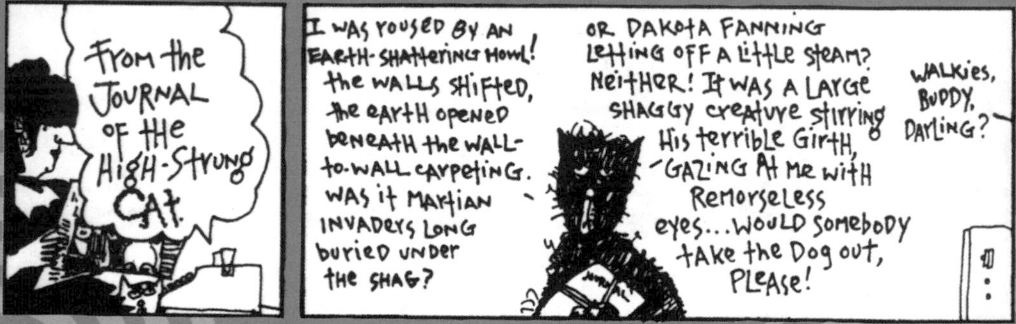

From the Journal of the High-Strung Cat.
I was roused by an earth-shattering howl! the walls shifted, the earth opened beneath the wall-to-wall carpeting. was it Martian invaders long buried under the shag?
or Dakota Fanning letting off a little steam? Neither! It was a large shaggy creature stirring His terrible Girth, gazing At me with Remorseless eyes... would somebody take the Dog out, please!
Walkies, Buddy, Darling?

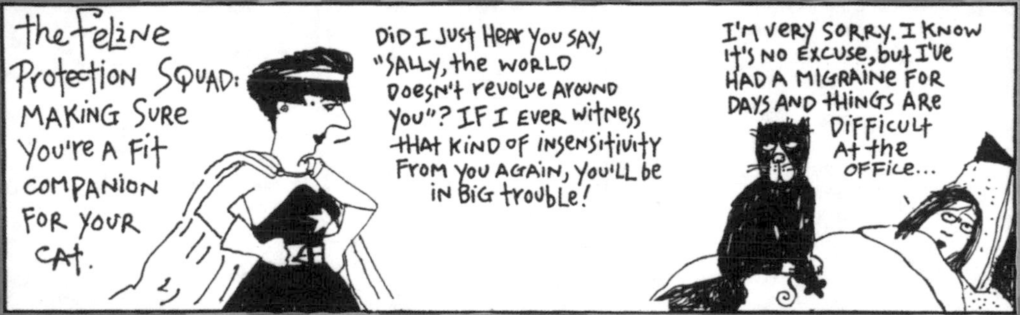
the Feline Protection Squad: MAKING SURE You're A Fit COMPANION FOR YOUR CAT.
DID I JUST HEAR YOU SAY, "SALLY, the WORLD DOESN'T revolve AROUND YOU"? IF I EVER witness THAT KIND OF INSENSITIVITY FROM YOU AGAIN, YOU'LL be IN BIG trouble!
I'M very SORRY. I KNOW it'S NO EXCUSE, but I'VE HAD A MIGRAINE FOR DAYS AND THINGS ARE DIFFICULT At the OFFICE...

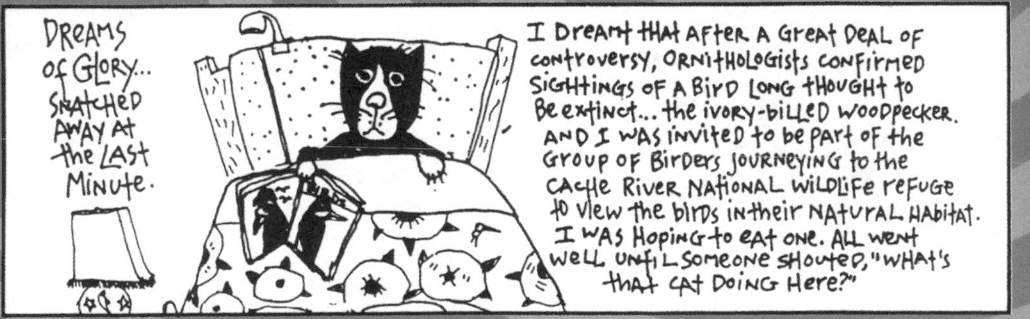
DREAMS OF GLORY... SNATCHED AWAY At the LAST Minute.
I Dreamt that After A Great Deal of controversy, ORNITHOLOGISTS CONFIRMED SIGHTINGS OF A BIRD LONG thought to Be extinct... the ivory-billed woodpecker. AND I WAS invited to be part of the Group of Birders journeying to the CACHE River NATIONAL WILDLIFE refuge to view the birds in their NATURAL HABITAT. I WAS Hoping to eat one. ALL went well until someone shouted, "WHAT'S that cat Doing Here?"

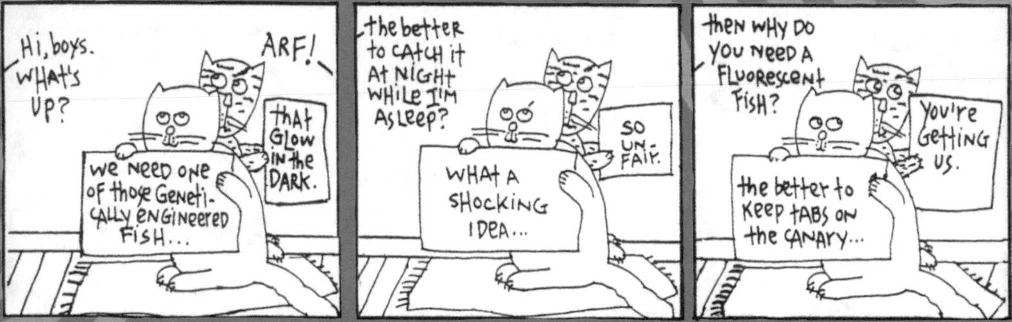
Hi, boys. WHAT's UP?
ARF!
we NEED ONE of those Geneti-cally ENGINeered FISH...
that GLOW in the DARK.
the better to CATCH it At NIGHT WHILE I'M ASLEEP?
WHAT A SHOCKING IDEA...
SO UN-FAIR.
then WHY DO YOU NEED A FLUORESCENT FISH?
the better to KEEP TABS ON the CANARY...
You're GettING US.

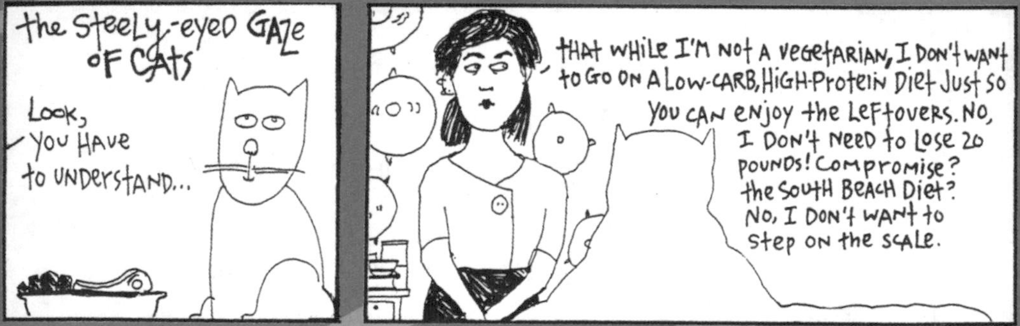
the Steely-eyed GAZe OF CATS
Look, YOU HAVE to UNDERSTAND...
THAT WHILE I'M NOT A VEGETARIAN, I DON'T WANT to GO ON A LOW-CARB, HIGH-Protein Diet Just so YOU CAN enjoy the LeftOVERS. NO, I DON'T NEED to Lose 20 POUNDS! Compromise? the SOUTH BEACH Diet? NO, I DON'T WANT to step ON the SCALE.

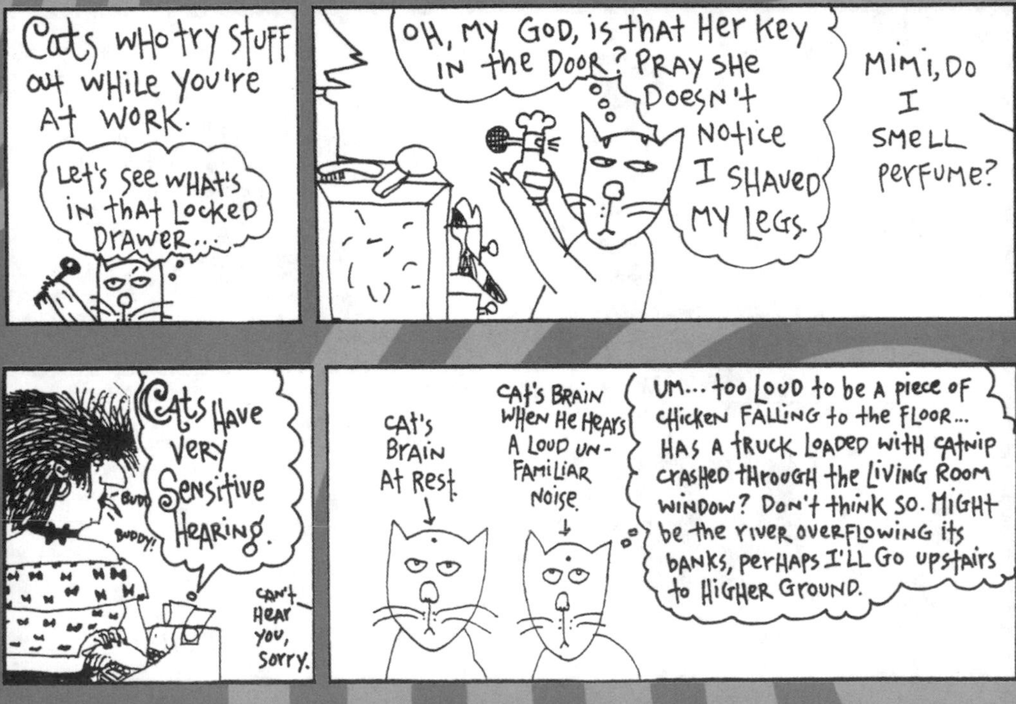
Cats WHO try STUFF out WHILE you're At WORK.
Let's see WHAT'S in thAt Locked DrAWer...
OH, MY GOD, is that Her key in the DOOR? PRAY SHE DOESN'T Notice I SHAVED MY LeGS.
MIMI, DO I SMELL perFUMe?
Cats HAVe VerY Sensitive Hearing.
BUDDY!
CAN'T HeAR YOU, SORRY.
CAT'S BRAIN At Rest.
CAT'S BRAIN WHEN He HEARS A LOUD UN-FAMILIAR NOISE.
UM... too LOUD to be A piece OF CHICKEN FALLING to the FLOOR... HAS A TRUCK LOADED WITH CATNIP CRASHED THROUGH the LIVING ROOM WINDOW? DON'T think SO. MIGHT be the river OVERFLOWING its BANKS, perHAPS I'LL GO UPSTAIRS to HIGHER GROUND.

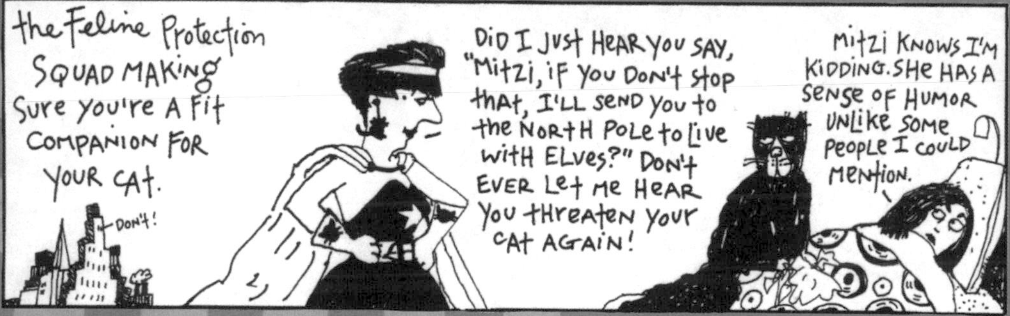
the Feline Protection SQUAD MAKING Sure you're A Fit COMPANION FOR YOUR CAT.
DON'T!
DID I JUST HEAR YOU SAY, "Mitzi, if you Don't stop that, I'LL SEND you to the NORTH POLE to Live with ELves?" Don't EVER Let me HEAR You tHREATEN your CAT AGAIN!
Mitzi KNOWS I'M KIDDING. SHE HAS A SENSE OF HUMOR UNLike some People I could mention.

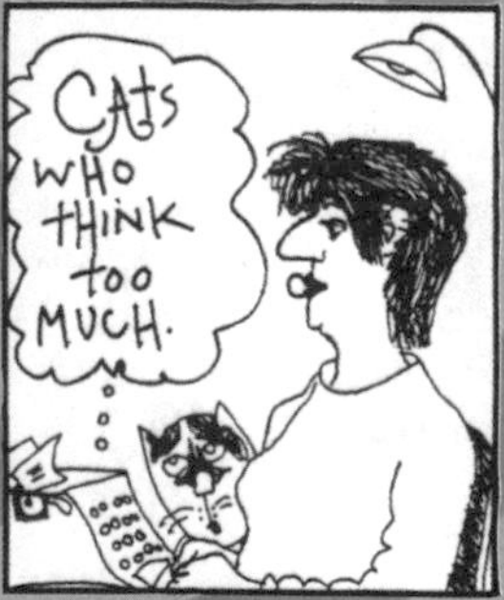
CATS WHO THINK too MUCH.

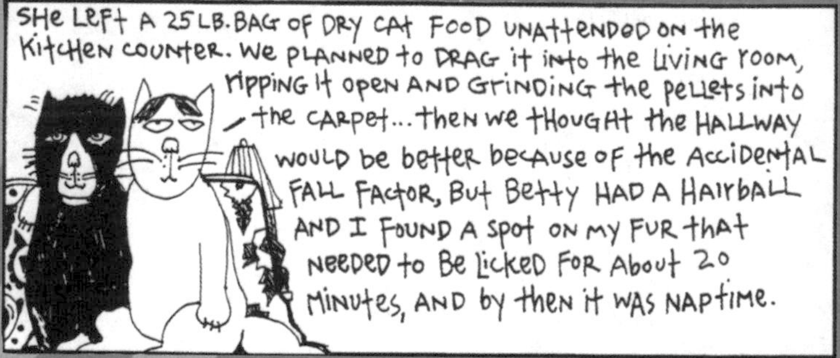
SHE LEFT A 25 LB. BAG OF DRY CAT FOOD UNATTENDED ON the Kitchen counter. We PLANNED to DRAG it into the Living room, ripping it open AND GRINDING the pellets into the carpet... then we thought the HALLWAY would be better because of the Accidental FALL Factor, But Betty HAD A HAIRBALL AND I FOUND A spot ON MY FUR that needed to Be Licked FOR About 20 Minutes, AND by then it WAS NAPtime.

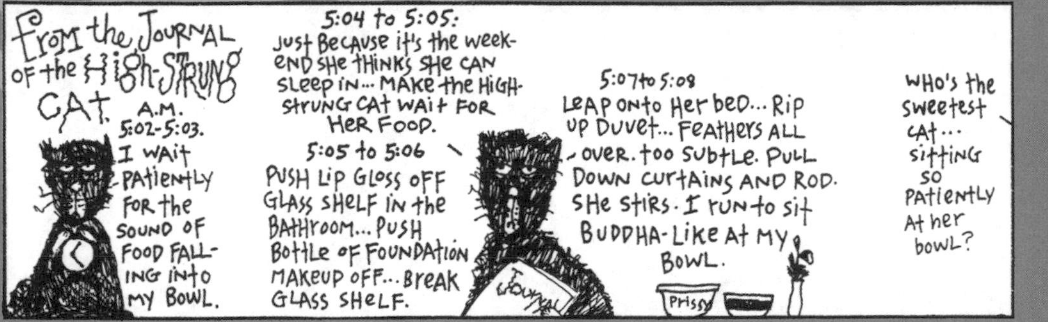
From the Journal of the High-Strung Cat
A.M. 5:02-5:03. I wait patiently for the sound of food falling into my bowl.
5:04 to 5:05: Just because it's the weekend she thinks she can sleep in... make the high-strung cat wait for her food.
5:05 to 5:06 Push lip gloss off glass shelf in the bathroom... push bottle of foundation makeup off... break glass shelf.
5:07 to 5:08 Leap onto her bed... rip up duvet... feathers all over. Too subtle. Pull down curtains and rod. She stirs. I run to sit Buddha-like at my bowl.
Who's the sweetest cat... sitting so patiently at her bowl?
Journal
Prissy

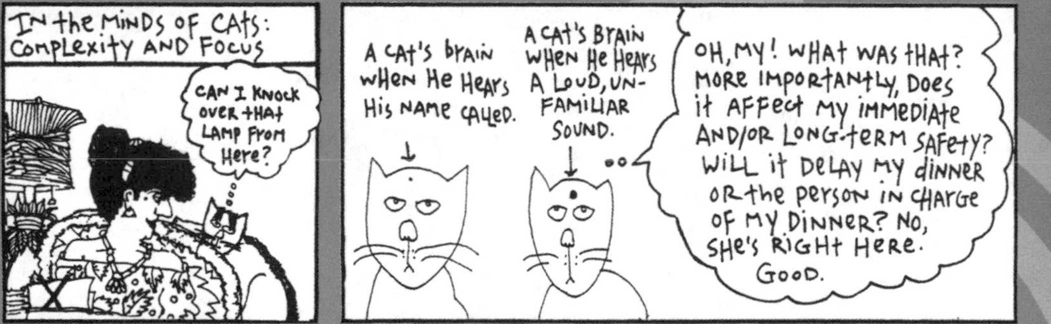
In the Minds of Cats: Complexity and Focus
Can I knock over that lamp from here?
A cat's brain when he hears his name called.
A cat's brain when he hears a loud, unfamiliar sound.
Oh, my! What was that? More importantly, does it affect my immediate and/or long-term safety? Will it delay my dinner or the person in charge of my dinner? No, she's right here. Good.

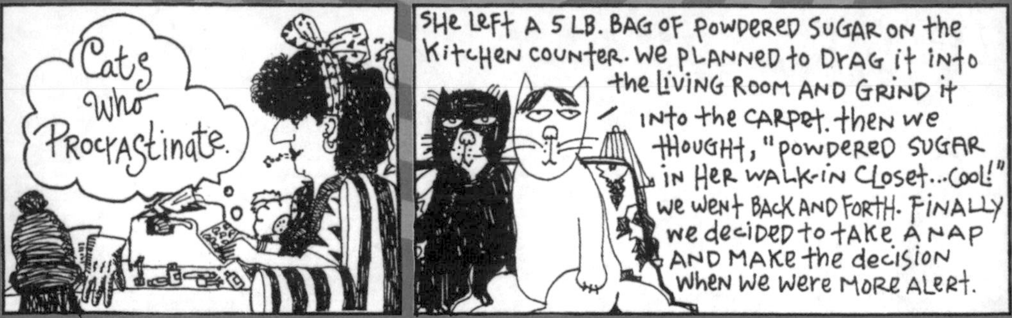
Cats who Procrastinate.
SHe left A 5 LB. BAG OF powdered SUGAR on the Kitchen counter. We planned to drag it into the living room and grind it into the carpet. then we thought, "powdered sugar in her walk-in closet...cool!" we went back and forth. Finally we decided to take a nap and make the decision when we were more alert.

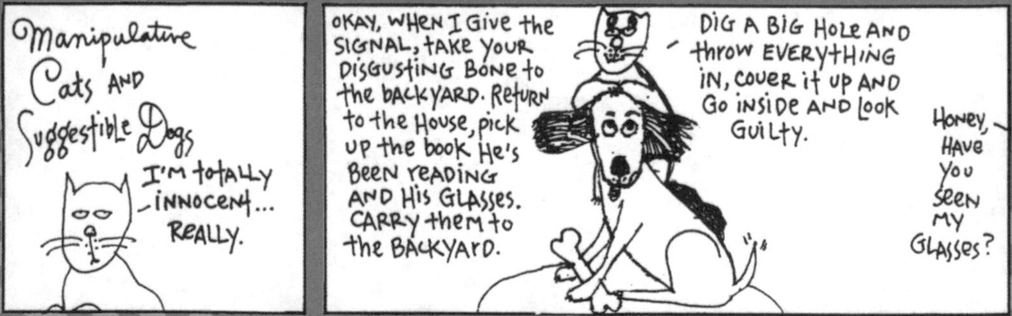
Manipulative Cats and Suggestible Dogs
I'm totally innocent... really.
Okay, when I give the signal, take your disgusting bone to the backyard. Return to the house, pick up the book he's been reading and his glasses. Carry them to the backyard.
Dig a big hole and throw everything in, cover it up and go inside and look guilty.
Honey, have you seen my glasses?

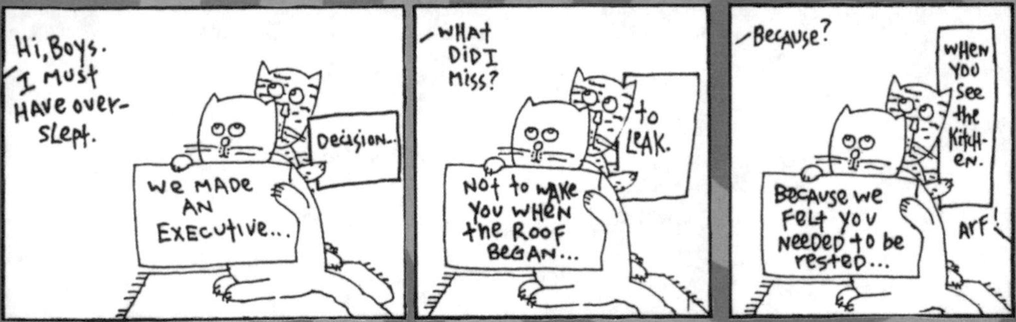
Hi, Boys. I must have over-slept.
We made an Executive...
Decision...
What did I miss?
Not to wake you when the Roof began...
to leak.
Because?
Because we felt you needed to be rested...
When you see the Kitchen.
ARF!

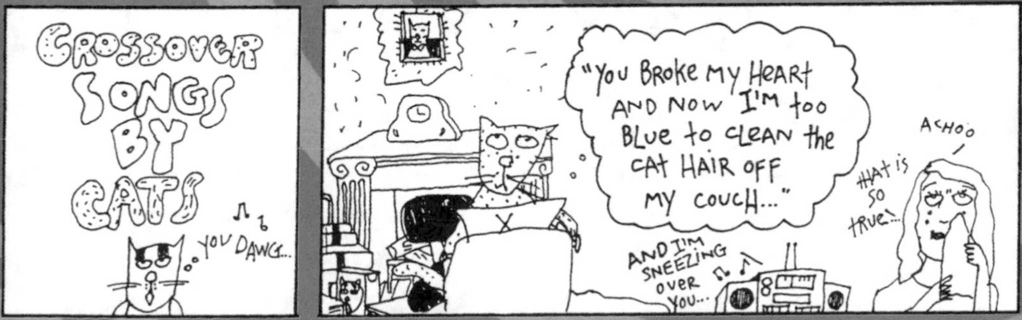
CROSSOVER SONGS BY CATS
You dawg...
"You Broke my Heart and now I'm too Blue to clean the cat Hair off my couch..."
AND I'M SNEEZING OVER YOU...
That is so true!...
ACHOO

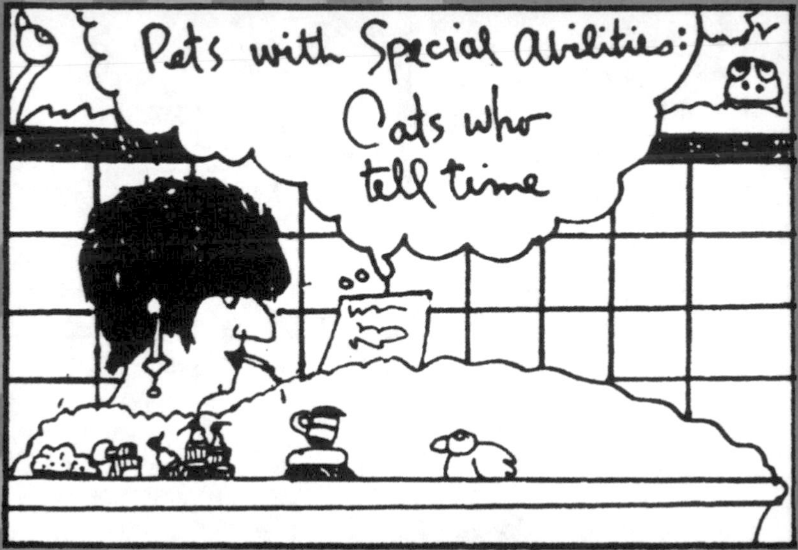
Pets with Special Abilities:
Cats who tell time

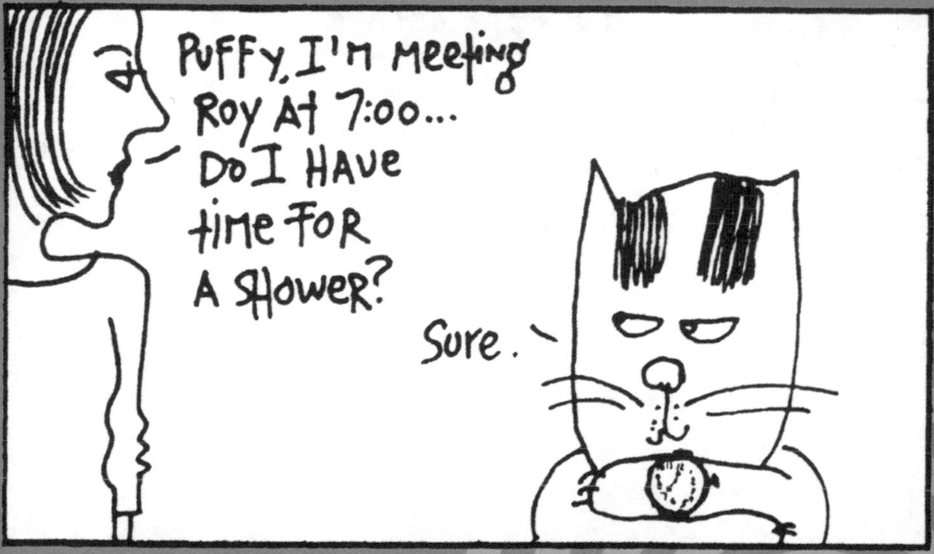
PUFFY, I'M MEETING ROY AT 7:00... DO I HAVE TIME FOR A SHOWER?
SURE.

ABOUT THE AUTHOR

Nicole Hollander is the author of the syndicated cartoon strip "Sylvia," which appears in sixty papers nationwide, including the *Chicago Tribune*, the *Boston Globe*, and the *Seattle Times.* Nicole lives in Chicago and shares her flat with two lovely pals, Buddy and Sally Cookie.